Geoffrey Knott is principal l̲e̲c̲t̲u̲r̲e̲r̲ ̲i̲n̲ ̲c̲h̲a̲r̲g̲e̲ ̲o̲f̲
the accountancy division, a̲t̲ ̲N̲o̲r̲w̲i̲c̲h̲ ̲C̲i̲t̲y̲ ̲C̲o̲l̲l̲e̲g̲e̲ ̲o̲f̲ ̲F̲u̲r̲t̲h̲e̲r̲
and Higher Education. On ̲t̲h̲e̲ ̲C̲o̲u̲n̲c̲i̲l̲ ̲o̲f̲ ̲t̲h̲e̲ ̲C̲h̲a̲r̲t̲e̲r̲e̲d̲
Association of Certified Ac̲c̲o̲u̲n̲t̲a̲n̲t̲s̲ ̲a̲n̲d̲ ̲A̲s̲s̲o̲c̲i̲a̲t̲i̲o̲n̲ ̲o̲f̲
Accounting Technicians, he has been closely connected with
the Business and Technician Education Council as a member
of the B2 Finance Board, of working parties for development of
accounting modules for BTEC courses, and of validation
committees for BTEC Higher National and Post-experience
accounting courses. He acts as a consultant management
accountant to businesses in East Anglia.

PAN MANAGEMENT GUIDES

Other books in the series:

PAN MANAGEMENT GUIDES

Management Accounting

Geoffrey Knott

Pan Original
Pan Books London and Sydney

First published 1986 by Pan Books Ltd,
Cavaye Place, London SW10 9PG
9 8 7 6 5 4 3 2 1
© Geoffrey Knott 1986
ISBN 0 330 29522 5
Photoset by Parker Typesetting Service, Leicester
Printed in Great Britain by
Richard Clay (The Chaucer Press) Ltd, Bungay, Suffolk

Contents

Introduction

In today's highly competitive national and international markets, it is imperative that businesses, large and small, make the most efficient use of scarce resources. If they do not, they may price themselves out of their markets, with the consequent loss of jobs and invested capital.

It follows that managers who plan and control operations should have ready access to relevant and timely information upon which to base their decisions. The provision of such information is the province of the management accountant.

Using the progressive stages of the management process as a framework, and without going into the detailed technicalities of accounting, this book examines and illustrates the concepts and techniques applied by the management accountant in the provision of management information.

The reader need have no prior knowledge of accounting to benefit from this book.

1 What is Management Accounting?

Decision-making and information

Each year, many people decide to go abroad for their annual holiday. They make the necessary travel, accommodation and other arrangements, and head for the sun.

They decide where to go after consulting holiday brochures and seeking advice from travel agents. They gather information about alternative holiday resorts, different modes and routes of travel, hotels at which to stay, foreign currency, travel insurance. Their eventual arrival on some exotic foreign shore is the culmination of a whole series of decisions made after consulting appropriate information.

Likewise, managers of business organizations operate by *making and carrying out decisions*, but to make those decisions they require information. Some of the information they require comes from *external* sources, e.g. prices charged by competitors, while a great deal of it is analysed and summarized by the *internal* management information system, e.g. costs of alternative production methods and estimates of future operating costs.

The provision of relevant financial and other information for managerial decision-making and control is the province of the management accountant.

The inadequacy of annual financial statements

At least once a year, most businesses produce financial information in the form of a balance sheet and a profit and loss account.

A balance sheet portrays on a particular date:

(a) the value of what a business owns, and
(b) who provided the finance for, and therefore owns, those assets.

The form and content of a simple Balance Sheet is shown below:

Balance sheet of Apex Engineers plc at 31 December 19....

	£000s	£000s
Fixed assets		
Land and buildings (net value)	110,000	
Machinery (net value)	50,000	160,000
Current assets		
Stock	45,000	
Debtors	25,000	
Cash	10,000	
	80,000	
Less current liabilities		
Creditors	40,000	40,000
Net asset value		£200,000
Financed by		
Share capital		60,000
Retained profit		100,000
Shareholders' capital		160,000
Long-term loan		40,000
		£200,000

Fixed assets are those resources acquired to be used in the business over a long period; *current assets* are those that will be converted into cash during a normal operational period – usually within a year. *Current liabilities* are amounts owing to short-term creditors and are usually payable within one year. Current assets less current liabilities is known as 'working capital'.

Share capital is the finance subscribed to the business by its owners from external sources; *retained profit* represents earnings from past operations reinvested in the business. It follows that the difference between the retained-profit figures between two balance-sheet dates is the profit remaining for that period after paying taxation and dividends.

The financial statement that shows how that profit is determined is the profit and loss account for the period, which normally contains the following essential details:

Apex Engineers plc
Profit and loss account for the year ended 31 December 19....

		£000s
Sales		550
less cost of goods sold		350
		200
Selling and distribution expenses	100	
Administration expenses	50	150
Net operating profit		50
Corporation tax		25
		25
Dividends paid		5
Retained profit for the year		20

The profit and loss account and balance sheet are the only financial information annually produced by thousands of organizations. But they report only *historical* figures, about the *whole* organization, and do very little to assist managers to plan for the *future*.

Long-term investment decisions can only be based upon the appraisal of *expected future cash flows*, while short-term decisions may only use *relevant* costs and revenues.

Neither of these information sets is to be found in historically prepared financial statements, although, to be fair, past performance and data can help to signpost the future and can be compared with *planned* performance if this is available.

The range and timing of management accounting information will, of course, be governed by the needs of management. We have to examine the management process to appreciate those needs.

The management process can be summarized:

- decide objectives
- plan strategy to achieve objectives
- install an efficient organization structure
- plan operations
- implement the plan
- control operations.

Objectives

Sir Freddie Laker and, more recently, Richard Branson, decided to enter the airline industry and, as entrepreneurs, they expected to earn a reasonable profit from their investment – at least in the long-term. They understood the risks involved, particularly competition from the major airlines, and they would not have risked their capital if they had thought the venture would not reward them for taking that risk.

To earn reasonable profits on capital invested in airline operations was, for both of them, their major *objective*, but this was supported by twin subsidiary objectives of high-quality service and low passenger fares.

As their businesses developed, the main profit objective remained but was joined by subsidiary objectives such as a specified growth target for the number of passengers carried. Immediately prior to liquidation, the major objective of Laker Airline was to survive.

All organizations must set out their objectives, long- and short-term, to justify their existence; this applies equally to both commercial and non-commercial operations.

Strategic Planning

The main functions of management are planning and controlling.

Planning is deciding what to do; controlling is carrying out and monitoring plans. *Strategic* planning involves decisions on how to achieve objectives – usually long-range plans, mainly concerning:

- what service or product to provide
- what customer group (or market) to provide for.

Richard Branson's Virgin Atlantic Airline initially chose to offer a cross-Atlantic, low-fare passenger service – with no frills. It will probably not be content to restrict operations to present services, however. Freight carrying, chartering aircraft to package-tour operators, extending operations to other routes and other classes of passenger, all beckon the ambitious airline operator.

In highly competitive markets, a business is forced into a process of reappraising its existing products and customers, and must be innovative if it is to survive. In manufacturing industry this is achieved by a programme of product research and development, governed by the rate of change in the particular industry. In the food and electronics industries, for instance, new products are constantly being marketed and fresh markets opened up. Strategic planners will, therefore, look to the management accountant to help them appraise the cash-flow consequences of alternative product and marketing strategies, choice of the optimum strategy, and consequent long-term investment and financing decisions.

Organizing

As a business expands and becomes more complex, its owner is unable to make and control all decisions as before, since he has neither time nor expertise. He then has to delegate authority to managers. In a manufacturing company, specialist managers would eventually head the major functional departments concerned with marketing, production, research and development, finance, and general administration and personnel; each function being divided further into specialist subdepartments with their own managers. Figure 1 shows an organization chart with lines of responsibility set out. Functional heads report direct to the managing director, while managers of subdepartments report to functional heads.

In addition to *line* relationships, some functions will serve several other functions on a formal or informal basis, e.g. management accounting will involve discussions with all other departments. These are *staff* rela-

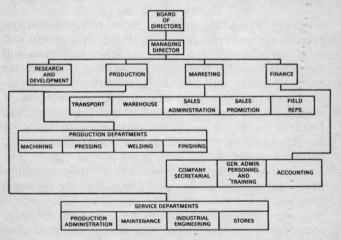

Figure 1. Organization chart for an engineering company

tionships. It is important not only to clarify the line and staff structure of the organization but also to lay down exact responsibilities and limits of authority for each manager of each subunit. This is best done by drawing up job descriptions for all of them. You will see the importance of this later when we deal with control by budgets.

Operational planning

The strategic plan is the grand design for the relatively long term, and provides the framework within which managers will operate and make necessary short-term decisions. The short-term here normally refers to a one-year period, the decisions for which are embodied in an operational budget or plan. Short-term decisions will be taken to cover such problems as resource acquisition, planned output volume, determining selling prices and arranging for temporary 'bridging' finance.

Implementing plans

Carrying out plans requires effective communications. We are dealing with people in organizations, not just machines and materials. The best laid of schemes will not come to fruition if the people to carry them out are not properly *directed, motivated, and co-ordinated*. Directing does not simply mean ordering people about; it involves a participative process to instruct what has to be done and why. People will generally collaborate far more willingly if they are consulted and will, indeed, contribute more.

Other motivating influences will include remuneration packages, working conditions and levels of job satisfaction.

It is at the implementation stage that all resources specified by the operational plan are co-ordinated so as to be in the right place at the right time.

Controlling

The essentials of all systems are input, processing and output. We put a coin into a ticket machine which 'triggers' an internal mechanism and eventually outputs a ticket. Manufacturers input resources into a process, conversion takes place and a finished product is output. But this is not all, for systems require information fed back to them to control deviations from plan. The internal mechanism of the ticket machine must be 'told' if a rogue coin has found its way into the slot.

Likewise, management information systems are designed to feed back information to unit managers, to enable them to control their operations and to take prompt remedial action if things are going off course.

Figure 2 summarizes the progressive steps in the management process.

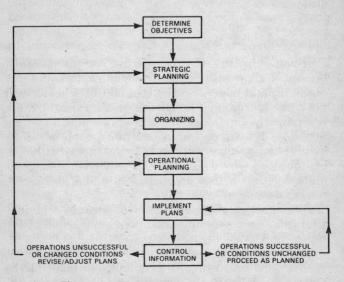

Figure 2. The management process

Management Accounting and the management process

In each of the stages of management discussed above, it was hinted that without *relevant* information, managers cannot function properly. The early stages of *strategic planning* will concern current 'state of the art' in product development, and consumer research. But appraisal of alternative strategies will eventually call for quantitative analysis, expressed largely in the common unit of money. The focus of this analysis will be on cash-flow timing over the long term, with a view to optimizing the value added to business wealth. This is dealt with in Chapter 4.

Determining the appropriate *organization structure* to carry through the chosen strategy has implications much wider than the concerns of accounting. Nevertheless, the management accountant needs to influence the development of the structure to ensure that designated managers are charged with the responsibility of achieving the objectives set for the areas under their control. In particular, the structure will affect whether managers are only responsible for costs (i.e. cost centres); or both costs and revenue (profit centres); or have a much wider influence on investment, revenue and costs (investment centres).

The acquisition of plant, machinery and buildings results from long-term strategic decisions; whereas acquisition of materials, manpower and services, fixing volumes of production, and setting selling prices, are short-term *operational decisions*.

Operational plans or budgets, usually set for one year, are a combination of long- and short-term decisions, and the management accountant is normally responsible for co-ordinating the preparation of these budgets in conjunction with unit managers. When published, they express the managerial objectives for the coming budget period, at least in quantitative terms. However, words can sometimes be more powerful than figures when setting targets of performance for managers. Qualitative factors, such as improving quality of output and industrial relations, may loom much larger in a hierarchy of a manager's objectives.

At *implementation* stage, the management accountant will mainly be concerned with systems design, to ensure that data recording and periodic reporting provide effective communications between all functional and service departments.

Output from the management accounting system will be in the form of periodic reports according to the *control* requirements of each segment of the organization. The frequency of reporting is governed by the need to take action. Daily reports may be produced to monitor labour losses, for example, while it might be adequate to control maintenance costs monthly. Each report should compare actual with planned activity, highlighting significant deviations from plan, with the ultimate object of taking appropriate corrective action, or changing the plan where necessary.

2 Cost Classification

INTRODUCTION

'Hello Paul, do sit down,' invited George Stubbs, management accountant of Hemming Agricultural Machinery Ltd.

Paul Hemming had recently joined his father's business after receiving a degree in agricultural engineering and was initially spending a short time in each department to obtain an overview of the company's operations.

Two weeks with the sales department had given him an introduction to the product range and to some of the problems of marketing, and now he wished to see what part the management accountant played in the firm.

'Accounting for costs is the largest part of my job, so we ought to give that our attention first,' began George, 'but a word of caution; the term "cost" has chameleon-like qualities, for while the layperson might restrict the word to meaning the amount of money paid for something, the businessman chooses to classify costs in different ways according to purpose.'

George then suggested that it would help if they put their discussion into a practical context and visited the finished goods warehouse.

Direct and indirect costs

Immediately inside the warehouse door were row upon row of electrically driven lawnmowers.

'They are R.20 models,' Paul ventured proudly.

'Quite right,' agreed George. 'Now, as a first exercise, can you identify some of the different materials and parts in the finished machine?'

Paul examined a mower and reeled off descriptions of each type of material and component.

George then explained that most of the list was classified as *direct materials*, being directly and easily traced to the mower. The small nuts, bolts and washers mentioned by Paul, although obviously part of the mower, were too small to be accounted for separately and were therefore described as *indirect materials*. There were many other materials used in production, e.g. machine oil, cleaning brushes and machine coolant, that were impossible to trace directly to any one product and were also classified as *indirect*.

'Similarly,' he went on, 'the wages of the men working directly on the production of each mower are referred to as *direct labour*; other labour that cannot be so readily identified with one product, such as the works manager's salary and expenses, being *indirect labour*.

'Further, the patent royalty paid to the designers of the special cutter blade is classified as a *direct expense* because it is specifically related to the R.20 mower; all other expenses, such as heating oil, power, rent, rates and staff restaurant subsidy, are incurred for the benefit of many products and are *indirect expenses*.

'The terms direct and indirect also apply to departmental cost analysis. For example, the maintenance manager's salary can be charged *directly* to the maintenance department and is therefore a *direct expense* of that department; whereas the heating costs of that department are an apportioned part of the total factory heating bill.

'The significance of the direct and indirect classification lies in the effort made to arrive at true cost. If all costs are direct, this objective is achieved. If most costs are indirect, we have to resort to some form of averaging to apportion them to products or departments.'

George then drew Figure 3 to illustrate his point.

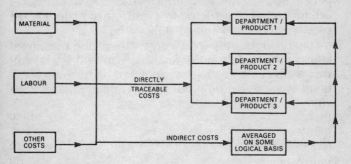

Figure 3. Composition of departmental/product cost

Expired and Unexpired costs

'What about costs of buildings, machinery and equipment?' asked Paul. 'These are acquired to be used in the business over an extended period of time; how are *they* reflected in product cost?'

'In a sense these are *pre-paid* resources,' George replied, 'because they will contribute to many years' production until their use value is completely exhausted. In accounting parlance they are *capital expenditure*, whereas expenditure on resources that will be used up in the short term is referred to as *revenue expenditure*. The latter will include materials used in current production, labour and most other expenses.

'For example, if we buy a jig-boring machine for £50,000 and expect it to operate efficiently for ten years, with no value remaining at the end of that time, we would charge £5,000 to each year's cost of production as an indirect cost classified as *depreciation*. At the end of each financial year the *unexpired value* of the machine appears as an asset in the balance sheet, the assumption being that the value shown represents its true future worth to the company.'

Paul asked if the same principle applied to purchases of sheet steel, electric motors and other materials not used in production immediately.

'Yes, it does,' replied George, 'the value of unused stocks of materials at the financial year end is also carried in the balance sheet as an asset, because they will be of value to future production. Only *expired costs* are charged to current production.'

Product costs and period costs

Paul produced a report showing a summary profit and loss account for the previous month relating to the lawnmower division of the company, as follows:

		£
Sales		120,360
Cost of sales		65,100
Gross profit		55,260
Selling expenses	19,280	
General administration expenses	10,500	
		29,780
Net profit		25,480

He pointed to the cost-of-sales figure and asked how that related to the cost of production.

George explained the need to carry stocks of finished lawnmowers to satisfy wholesalers' orders without delay; this meant that production had to be ahead of sales. Cost of goods sold in a month comprised opening stock plus cost of production, less stock at the end of the month. That is, only *product manufacturing cost* is included in cost of sales.

'However, selling and administration costs are all charged against the profit of the period in which they are incurred, no part of them being carried forward as value of unsold stocks. They are deemed to relate only to the goods sold in the month and are known as *period costs*.'

Volume of activity and cost

Paul queried whether some product costs were not also period costs. As an example, he suggested that factory rent and rates covered a period of time rather than a particular volume of output. They are incurred whatever the output volume, so shouldn't they be wholly charged to the period and not included as part of the value of stock?

George agreed that, in essence, Paul was correct. But he explained that most manufacturers include all factory costs, including fixed period costs, as part of product cost; otherwise stock would be undervalued.

'For *decision-making purposes*, however, it is important to analyse how costs are affected by changes in volume of activity, and in anticipation of this topic arising I have drafted this schedule.'

George showed Paul the following figures:

Fixed costs	£1,000	1,000	1,000	1,000	1,000	1,000
Units produced	200	300	400	500	600	700
Costs per unit:						
Fixed	5.00	3.33	2.50	2.00	1.67	1.43
Variable	2.00	2.00	2.00	2.00	2.00	2.00
Total	7.00	5.33	4.50	4.00	3.67	3.43

'Notice how fixed cost per unit *varies* with changes in volume of output, while variable cost per unit is *fixed*.

Changes in total fixed and variable costs could happen at higher output levels but, within the illustrated range of output, unit cost is progressively reduced because fixed costs are spread over an increasing number of units.'

'I can see how vital it is, in our highly competitive market, to maintain full-capacity working,' Paul observed.

'Exactly,' agreed George, 'but knowledge of cost behaviour goes beyond this. It can help us to (a) forecast what profit to expect at different levels of output; (b) decide whether to accept an order at less than full cost – when we are working below full capacity; and (c) decide whether to make or buy a machine part.'

Future costs for decision-making

'Decisions concern the future,' George continued, 'therefore we have to *forecast* the costs to include in our calculations. Past costs may be a guide to the future but, beyond this, they are irrelevant in the context of decision-making. They are "water under the bridge".

'For example, our stock of lawnmower throttle handles may have been purchased for £3 each two months ago but, if *replacement cost* is now £4, that is the value to use in a current cost estimate.

'Decision-making costs do not just include variable cost per unit. If we were considering whether to make a part rather than to buy it, we might have to purchase additional machinery – a so-called fixed cost. But in the context of this decision, the machinery would be an additional or *incremental cost* and has to be taken into account.

'A little more obscurely, future costs must also take account of any income foregone as a result of using an existing resource for some other purpose. These are known as *opportunity costs*. For example, in a make or buy decision, if we are currently leasing a building to a farmer that could be used to manufacture a part that is presently bought in, the rental given up would be a lost opportunity and, therefore, a cost of making rather than buying.'

Cash flow and cost

'While it is important to appreciate the relevance of future costs in making decisions, it is just as important to recognize when those costs are actually paid for,' George went on.

'Machinery purchased for long-term use is normally paid for when it is installed, but accounted for, as depreciation, as it is used. Material might be bought and used immediately but paid for much later. Perhaps more significantly, we sell a large volume of machines overseas on long-term credit terms. Payment is sometimes delayed for two years.

'The significance of recognizing the *timing of cash flow* is that, as money has a time value, in the form of interest, early cash inflows are more valuable than those received later. This is particularly important in long-term investment appraisal, when we have to forecast cash flows for a number of years.'

3 Different Costs for Different Purposes

INTRODUCTION

Chapter 2 showed that costs can be classified in various ways. In this chapter we identify which cost classifications apply to the various purposes for which we need to know cost. No one concept is universally applicable; cost being the *relevant value* of resources used or planned to be used for a particular purpose. The operative word being 'relevant'.

As the management process dictates the purposes for which information is required, the linking of cost classification and purpose follows the progressive planning and control stages of that process.

Cost information for long-term, strategic decisions

Strategic planning must be based upon attainable objectives. There is little point in setting a higher target for return on capital invested if *external* and *internal* influences affecting the organization render the target unrealistic. An expected recession in the industry may render impossible any improvement in profit in the short term. Similarly, charities with ambitions to expand their activities have to set objectives within their capacities to raise funds.

Plans may therefore be laid for relatively restricted objectives which simply aim at *improving* existing products and their markets.

A more ambitious profit objective might be considered if there is considerable scope for *expansion* of an existing product range or of the markets in which a business presently sells. Even if these strategies are ruled out because no further development of products or markets is possible, a wider policy of diversification could be followed.

Diversifying means engaging in another activity. For example, the Imperial Group (Imps) have interests in many activities and products that have no direct connection with the group's original industry – tobacco. Companies that engage in such a diversity of interests, partly to reduce overall risk, are called *conglomerates*, and are at one extreme of diversifiction. At the other extreme, a company manufacturing shoes might diversify *vertically*, to protect its sources of supply or markets, by buying interests in leather tanning (a previous process) or in shoe retailing (the following process).

Whatever strategy is adopted, *maximization of the value of future cash flows* is the major concept applied.

Consider two mutually exclusive projects, A and B, forecast to yield the following total profits over five years:

	A	B
Sales	100,000	100,000
Cost of sales	50,000	45,000
Profit	£ 50,000	55,000

Project B appears to be the more profitable but if the B customer is allowed two years' extended credit and A has to pay within one month of delivery, Project A begins to look more attractive because its earlier cash flows can be invested before those of B.

In addition, if B's cost of sales includes a machine costing £15,000 which has to be paid for immediately after its installation, whereas A's cash flows are concen-

trated into years three, four and five, A could well be
more profitable than B.

Use of discounted cash-flow techniques would help
solve this problem and these will be examined more
closely in Chapter 4.

Although cash flow predominates in the evaluation of
long-term investment proposals, the analysis will have
to recognize the *behaviour of costs* (e.g. fixed/variable)
and, in particular, that only *future costs* are relevant.

Cost accumulation for operational planning and control

The short-term operational plans of a business are
expressed in the form of *budgets* – usually for the year
ahead – and they serve two fundamental purposes:

- as action 'blueprints' to guide those responsible for
  resourcing operations for the coming year
- as monitoring devices against which to check
  actual performance during and at the end of the
  year

At the very least they will comprise budgets of profit
and loss, capital expenditure and cash for the coming
year, and a balance sheet at the end of that year.

In a multi-product enterprise, the profit and loss
budget will be broken down further into product
groups, usually referred to as *'profit'* or *'investment'*
centres. This subdivision enables control to be exercised
over the activities and costs of each centre by comparing
actual with budgeted performance.

It follows that the same system and classification of
costs and revenues will apply to both the compilation of
budgets and to the subsequent recording of actual performance. If this was not so, the control function of
budgets would be meaningless.

The cost concept absolutely central to the compilation of the profit and loss account, is that of including *expired costs* only. These are the *product costs* of the goods sold, plus selling and administration period costs. Recall that the *unexpired value* of resources such as buildings, machinery and stock is carried forward to future periods.

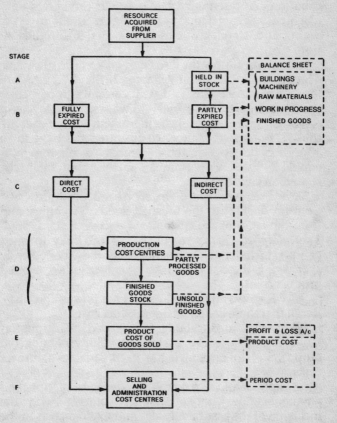

Figure 4. Flow of resources through a manufacturing company

Figure 4 (page 29) traces the flow of resources through a manufacturing company.

Stage A shows resources 'held in stock', that is, for use over more than one period, and includes buildings, machinery and raw materials.

Stage B points to the resources transferred into the production and selling functions; the partly expired contribution representing that part of buildings and machinery estimated to have been used up (i.e. depreciation) and raw materials issued to production from stock.

Stage C introduces the *direct* and *indirect* classifications of costs. As explained in Chapter 2, the *direct costs* are those that can be allocated with certainty to particular cost centres, e.g. the salaries and wages of employees in each cost centre can easily be identified. *Indirect costs* are those serving two or more cost centres and have to be apportioned between those centres, using the most equitable basis. For example, factory rent might be shared on an area basis.

Stage D shows *expired product costs* being transferred from production to the finished goods warehouse and from the latter to the customer, i.e. cost of goods sold. The *unexpired product cost* of partly and fully finished goods is included in the balance sheet at the period end.

Stage E is the cost of finished goods sold (i.e. expired product costs).

Stage F shows *expired* selling and administration costs. Recall that these are *period* not product costs.

When constructing budgets it is particularly important to relate the level of costs to the volume of budgeted output, i.e. to recognize the fixed/variable nature of costs.

As explained in Chapter 2, the *timing* of receipts and payments does not necessarily coincide with the inclusion of the associated sales and expired costs in the profit and loss account. Consequently, a cash budget must also be prepared to monitor against actual cash flows.

Costs and selling prices

In the long run, selling prices must cover all costs, however they are classified, otherwise capital will be eroded.

For example, oil companies will not invest in the development of new oilfields if they judge that the future price of oil will not cover development, capital, operating costs, taxes and a reasonable profit on their capital investment.

In other circumstances, however, the market-given price may be attractive enough for a firm to enter the market or to remain in it. The question is – what level of output will optimize profit? The answer must be – that volume at which the margin between total sales and total costs is greatest.

This will entail an analysis of *incremental costs* at progressively higher levels of output, recognizing that additional *fixed* as well as *variable* costs will be incurred.

When a firm is a price maker rather than a price taker, full-cost formulas similar to the following are used:

	per unit
	£
Manufacturing cost:	
direct	50
indirect	40
	90
Selling and administration	20
	110
Add profit, say 10%	11
	121

In circumstances where a firm is working at less than full capacity, full cost is irrelevant to pricing – at least in the short term. In these conditions, *variable cost* will be the minimum price to charge, any amount recoverable over that being a *contribution* towards fixed costs and profit.

More will be said about pricing in Chapter 11.

Costs for short-term decisions

At the end of the last section, we saw that relevant cost for short-term pricing is variable cost.

The same principle of *incremental* or *out-of-pocket* cost also applies in many other short-term circumstances.

For example, analysis may show that a product sells at a loss as follows:

		£
Selling price		20
less direct cost	15	
share of indirect cost	7	
	—	22
		—
Loss		2
		—

Should the product be discontinued? The answer is that, if no better use can be made of the facilities producing the item, it should be retained because it is making *a contribution* to fixed costs and profit of £20 − £15 = £5.

In short, when deciding between alternatives *the relevant costs are those which differ between the alternatives.* Past costs and committed costs are irrelevant.

We look into this decision-making area in more detail in Chapter 10.

4 Long-term Capital Investment Decisions

INTRODUCTION

A group of companies operating predominantly in the hotel industry, but with interests in casinos and food processing, announced it was selling its food-processing division. Its directors had probably decided that all economic and social indicators point to leisure as a growth industry of the future and, since the group's expertise lies mainly in this more profitable area, it should concentrate its resources accordingly.

The change of direction will enable the group to set a higher profit objective, which will ward off potential take-over predators.

In pursuance of its revised objective and chosen strategy, the group will sell its food-processing division, then evaluate alternative investment projects concerned with acquiring and building hotels with a view to selecting the optimum package of new projects and continuing activities which it is hoped will achieve the group's revised objectives.

This example illustrates that investment decisions stem out of the strategy chosen to achieve business objectives, which are themselves subject to external and internal constraints.

External influences include the forecast economic and political climate, technological developments, competition and expectations of investors, affecting the availability of finance. Internal constraints include the present state of new product development, sales forecasts for existing products, forecast cash flows and the capacity of management to cope with change.

Investment projects can be grouped under three main headings:

- replacement of plant and machinery
- expansion of existing and new products or services into existing or new areas
- diversification into related processes/industries or into completely different ones.

Essence of investment appraisal

Investment is the process of committing finance otherwise available for consumption, to a project which is expected to recover the capital invested within the anticipated life of the project, together with an additional return to compensate for the operational and time risks involved.

For example, an individual investor might purchase a £1,000, one-year 12% building society bond. He does so knowing that he will receive £120 interest during the year and his capital returned at the end of the year. Another investor might choose to invest £1,000 in a 5 year 13% government stock. He would receive £130 per annum and the return of his £1,000 at the end of five years. In each case, consumption of £1,000 has been deferred and interest received to compensate for the waiting period and risk involved. The longer period investment attracts a higher rate of interest because of the added time risk.

Investment in business is very similar, excepting that the timing of the cash flows would not be known with such certainty. Capital outlay on machinery, etc., might be spread over two or three years and typically, net cash inflow might follow a pattern of low initial yields, building up a maximum as the project attains its highest potential, then keeping to a plateau until returns start to wane. The project would be terminated when it reached the end of its natural life or when another investment opportunity promised a marginally higher return. The initial capital invested is thus recouped out of annual net cash inflows during, rather than at the end of, the project's life, with the balance of the cash flows meeting the higher return expected from a more risky business venture.

Thus, the essential characteristics of most business investment decisions are:

- an initial capital outlay
- an estimated life for the project
- a series of cash flows
- a required rate of return related to the risk of the project.

The investment finance will be obtained either from the existing owners of the business or by borrowing from outsiders. The sources of finance and the calculation of its cost are not the province of this book, but for appraisal purposes a cost of capital is assumed.

An accounting approach to investment decisions

The forecast cash flows from two alternative investments of £4,000 are scheduled below:

Both investments appear to yield the same return of 16.6%, but a closer examination shows B's cash flows to be greater in the early years. They would therefore be preferred because they could be reinvested sooner.

A simple arithmetic average of expected profits is not an acceptable criterion on which to base investment decisions, because it ignores the timing of cash flows and the fact that money has a time value.

Year	Project A £	Project B £
1	1,000	3,000
2	2,000	2,000
3	3,000	1,000
	6,000	6,000
Less capital outlay	4,000	4,000
Net profit	2,000	2,000
Average profit per annum	666	666
Average profit % of capital invested	16.6%	16.6%

The time value of money

If you were offered the alternative of receiving £1 now or in one year's time, you would doubtless opt for payment now. Quite apart from the frustration of having to wait for your money, you calculate that £1 received now and reinvested at 10% would be worth £1.10 in one year. You would be indifferent between receiving £1 now and £1.10 in a year's time. Ten pence is the time value of the one-year delay.

Should you have to wait a further year, what amount would you be prepared to accept then in lieu of £1 now? The answer is £1.10 plus 10% interest for one year, i.e. £1.21.

This can be written as a simple equation:

$$A = P \times (1+i) \times (1+i)$$
$$\text{or } A = P(1+i)n = P(1+i)^n$$

where A = the sum received at a future date
$\quad$ P = the amount invested now
$\quad\,$ i = the rate of interest
$\quad$ n = the number of years p is invested

$$\text{thus } A = 1 \times (1.10) \times (1.10)$$
$$\text{or } A = 1(1.10)^2$$
$$A = £1.21$$

From this compound interest equation we can deduce that $P = \dfrac{A}{(1+i)n}$ where P is the present value of a sum receivable in the future at a stated rate of interest. For example, the present value of £1.21 receivable in two years' time at 10% interest is $\dfrac{1.21}{(1.10)^2} = £1$.

It follows that we can calculate the present value of £1 receivable any number of years hence at any rate of interest, as the Appendix at the end of this book illustrates. This enables us to express any series of cash flows to a common base of present value, and thus make comparison between alternative investment returns.

Applying present value to investment decisions

Using the cash flows in the example in the last section, and assuming a 10% required rate of return, the comparative figures for Projects A and B are:

Year	PV factor at 10%	Cash flows A	B	Present values A £	B £
0	1.000	−4,000	−4,000	−4,000	−4,000
1	.909	+1,000	+3,000	+ 909	+2,727
2	.826	+2,000	+2,000	+1,652	+1,652
3	.751	+3,000	+1,000	+2,253	+ 751
Net present value				+ 814	+1,130

which confirms B as the more profitable project, *because it recovers the capital invested and adds £1,130− 814 =£316 more than A to the value of the business.*

The presumption in this example is that A and B are *mutually exclusive* investments. This could arise if capital is restricted, or if A and B are alternative ways of achieving the same operational objectives, e.g. they may be alternative machines. Viewed as independent projects with no constraints on available finance, they are both acceptable because they both yield positive net present values when discounted at the company's cost of capital. It follows that investments yielding negative NPV's should be rejected.

Relevant cash flows

Applying discounted cash flow (DCF) techniques to project appraisal is essential, but the arithmetic is relatively simple. Assessment of the different cash flows to include in the appraisal is far more important. In this section we look at various aspects concerning timing and relevance.

Assumption of end-year cash flows

Inherent in DCF is the assumption that all cash flows occur at the end of a year – this is because the table of factors is end-year calculated. The true pattern of receipts and payments, both capital and revenue, will vary from project to project but will generally be continuous rather than discretely end-year.

Given the long lives and uncertain cash flows of most projects, this will probably not significantly affect the investment decision. Short-life and high-value projects may warrant a more exact discounting approach, when monthly or even shorter period discounting factors should be applied.

Cash flow – not profit!

You will recall that profit is measured by deducting from the sales of a period the costs expired during that period. The accounting principle is one of matching against the sales realized in a period, the expenditure incurred in earning those sales. Expenditure includes depreciation – that part of the value of fixed assets used up during the period, and other product and period costs – regardless as to whether they have been paid for during the period.

When evaluating proposed investments using DCF techniques, we use cash-flow, not profit-measuring, principles. The initial outflow of cash for the purchase of buildings, and plant and machinery is recorded, but depreciation of those assets is not included in annual cash flows.

Consequential cash flows

Only cash flows that will occur because an investment decision is made, are included. Committed costs, such as rent of existing buildings and salaries of present supervisors, are not relevant. If new premises have to be leased and supervisors engaged arising out of a new investment project, these are *incremental* cash flows to be taken into account in the years in which they occur.

Similarly, the proceeds of sale of a replaced machine are part of the cash flow when evaluating the replacement machine, as are the proceeds of the sale of the new machine.

Opportunity cash flows

A department store was considering opening a restaurant in its store, as a customer service. There would be some capital expenditure on kitchen equipment and furniture, and it is expected that the restaurant will operate at a loss. Also, because the restaurant will be sited on the top floor, it will take up some furniture display floor space and consequently result in lost contribution from that department.

This lost opportunity must feature in the restaurant project appraisal, together with any net cash-flow gain resulting from additional general sales.

This example illustrates that both directly and indirectly affected cash flows may be relevant to a single investment project.

DCF example 1

Hemming Agricultural Machinery Ltd were considering adding a small weeding implement to their product range. Sufficient capacity was currently available to cope with the additional production, but an extra special-purpose machine costing £40,000 would have to be acquired and paid for immediately prior to commencement of production. The machine could be traded in at the end of year five for £5,000.

A new sales promotion programme would be mounted to market the new product and this would cost £10,000 at the commencement of production and £5,000 at the end of the first year.

The management accountant produced the following forecast figures relating to the proposed new product:

Year	Sales	Variable cost	Fixed cost
	£	£	£
1	52,000	30,000	23,000
2	78,000	47,000	28,000
3	100,000	65,000	30,000
4	60,000	35,000	24,000
5	36,000	19,000	20,000

Fixed costs includes £5,000 per annum for an additional part-time supervisor, £7,000 per annum depreciation on the machine and the balance an apportionment of existing costs. It can be assumed that no credit is given to customers or received from suppliers.

If the new product is accepted, it would take up facilities that could be used for another purpose to generate a net cash flow of £8,000 per annum.

The board of directors have asked the management accountant to submit an appraisal of the project covering a five-year period. Assume a cost of capital of 10%.

Solution

Year	0	1	2	3	4	5	Total
Marketing expense	(10,000)	(5,000)					
New machine	(40,000)						
Net cash earnings		17,000	26,000	30,000	20,000	12,000	←
Opportunity cost		(8,000)	(8,000)	(8,000)	(8,000)	(8,000)	
Net cash flow	(50,000)	4,000	18,000	22,000	12,000	9,000	
PV factor at 10%	1.000	.909	.826	.751	.683	.621	
Net present value	(50,000)	3,636	14,868	16,522	8,196	5,589	(1,189)

(handwritten annotations: sales − var costs − 5000 p.a.)

NOTES:

1 As the project has a negative NPV of £1,189, it should be rejected (but see later where the same project is adjusted for taxation and inflation).

2 Net cash earnings is sales less variable cost and £5,000 additional supervision.

3 Project cash flows might have to be adjusted for any credit allowed to customers or received from suppliers.

4 Apportioned fixed costs are irrelevant because they will be incurred whether this project goes ahead or not (depreciation is not cash flow), but the incremental expense of £5,000 for the part-time supervisor is relevant.

5 Value of alternative use of existing facilities, £8,000, is foregone and therefore treated as an opportunity cost.

Inflation

One of the uncertainties of forecasting cash flows is the effect of changing price levels. For example, if inflation is currently running at 10% per annum, £110 received in one year's time will buy no more than £100 now. Furthermore, if an investment of £100 returns £110 at the end of one year, with inflation at 10%, the nominal rate of return is 10%, but the real rate is zero. Should we then schedule cash flows in present-day or in future £s?

To answer this we must consider the discounting rate rather than cash flows.

The required rate of return represents the cost of finance – the rate required by the providers of that finance. It will include an element to compensate investors for waiting, i.e. delaying consumption of their wealth; an element to compensate the operational risk in the project; and a further increment to cover the expected fall in value of money during the period of the investment.

As the cost of capital is the applied discounting rate and includes inflation, it will be correctly matched if the forecast cash flows of an investment are stated in pounds, i.e. the actual number of pounds expected to flow. Cash flows must therefore anticipate inflation.

Moreover, if different elements of cost are subject to differing rates of price changes, cash flows must be adjusted accordingly. If wages are expected to increase by 12% for example, when the general price level is increasing by only 6%, it is the actual money wages paid that are included in cash flows.

Taxation

Business investment is made for profit, which, in most countries, is taxable. In addition, under most tax regimes, fixed assets, such as machinery, attract tax relief and therefore reduce tax paid. In both respects, cash flow is affected.

As UK corporation tax on the profits of each year is normally paid during the following year, and the effect of capital allowances on purchase of fixed assets is similarly delayed, cash flows are adjusted accordingly.

For example, supposing capital of £10,000 is invested in machinery which yields a net cash flow for each of four years, of £4,000. Assuming 30% corporation tax, and an allowance of 25% per annum on the original cost of the machinery the cash flows would appear as follows:

Year	Machine	Cash flow	Corporation tax	Net cash flow
	£	£	£	£
0	(10,000)			(10,000)
1		4,000	—	4,000
2		4,000	(450)	3,550
3		4,000	(450)	3,550
4		4,000	(450)	3,550
5			(450)	(450)

handwritten annotation:

$4000 \times .25 = 1000$
$3000 \times .25 = 750$
$2000 \times .25 =$
$1000 \times .25 = 250$
$\underline{\qquad}$
2500

NOTES:

1 Year 0 is the beginning of year 1.
2 The tax payable on profits, less each year's capital allowance, is £4,000 − 2,500 = 1,500 × 30% = £450.
3 Payment of tax is delayed by one year.
4 The fourth year's tax is payable in year 5.
5 Net cash flows would then be subject to discounting.

Should a business not be in a tax-paying position in the foreseeable future, perhaps because it has unrelieved losses or capital allowances brought forward from previous years, the taxation aspects of cash flows can be ignored until the business is in a tax-paying position once more.

DCF example 2

This is a continuation of DCF Example 1 adjusted for the effects of taxation and inflation. It is assumed that net cash earnings are subject to a compound rate of inflation of five per cent per annum over the five-year period, all other figures remaining the same, as in the first illustration, save for the imposition of taxation. In this respect the following assumptions are made:

a corporation tax of 30% is payable on profits
b 25% of the machine cost is allowed against profit in each of the first four years
c tax payment is delayed by one year.

The cost of capital remains at 10%.

17000 × 1.05; 26000 × 1.05²; 30,000 × 1.05³ etc

Solution

Year	0	1	2	3	4	5	6	NPV
				£s				
Marketing expense	(10,000)	(5,000)						
Net cash earnings		17,850	28,665	34,729	24,310	15,315		
Opportunity cost		(8,000)	(8,000)	(8,000)	(8,000)	(8,000)		
	(10,000)	4,850	20,665	26,729	16,310	7,315		
Corporation tax 30%			1,545	(6,200)	(8,019)	(4,893)	(2,195)	
	(10,000)	4,850	22,210	20,529	8,291	2,422	(2,195)	
New machine	(40,000)					5,000		
Tax allowance on machine			3,000	3,000	3,000	3,000	(1,500)	
	(50,000)	4,850	25,210	23,529	11,291	10,422	(3,695)	
PV rate @ 10%	1.000	.909	.826	.751	.683	.621	.564	
Present Value	(50,000)	4,409	20,823	17,670	7,712	6,472	(2,084)	5,002

(handwritten) delayed by 1 yr.

(handwritten) TAX PAYABLE ON TRADE IN VALUE

NOTES:

1 The NPV is now *positive* at £5,002 and therefore the project is acceptable. The decision is reversed (a) because operating cash flows have been adjusted for inflation, and (b) because of the net effect of taxation.
2 The net cash earnings figures in Example 1 have been adjusted for inflation as follows: Year 1 × 1.05; Year 2 × $(1.05)^2$; Year 3 × $(1.05)^3$; Year 4 × $(1.05)^4$; Year 5 × $(1.05)^5$.
3 Payment of corporation tax at 30% is delayed by one year.
4 Writing down allowance on the machine is £40,000 × 30% in total – spread over four years with a delayed impact.
5 Corporation tax is payable on the trade-in value of the machine i.e. £5,000 × 30% – delayed until year 6.
6 Figures in brackets indicate minus cash flows.

5 Accounting for Risk

What is risk?

What makes a government security relatively less risky than a share in an electronic company? The answer is that the government guarantees both payment of interest and repayment of capital on its securities, whereas dividend on an electronic share is much more volatile and there is no surety that the amount invested will be returned. The more variable the returns on an investment, the higher the probability of loss and the more risky the investment.

Peering into an uncertain future, the investment decision-maker must attempt to quantify risk and match it against his preference for risk. In any case, if the promised return does not compensate for the assessed risk, the investment ought not to go ahead.

The risk of an investment project will be subject to four main influences:

- *the time factor* – cash flows in the distant future are normally more uncertain than earlier ones
- *the type of project* – machine replacement decisions are normally less risky than new product expansion; investing in relatively stable food processing will not be as risky as the more volatile oil industry
- *business environmental risk* – including customer demand, reaction of competitiors, current industry trends, general economic and political factors both at home and overseas
- *how much the business is at risk currently* – a new project may not carry much risk in itself, but may

add to risk considerably when combined with operations of a similar nature.

This chapter examines some of the ways in which risk may be analysed and incorporated into the investment decision.

Payback

The following cash-flow forecasts relate to A and B, two alternative new products in a high-risk industry. A, with its higher NPV, is the more profitable. Both cash flows have been discounted at 10%.

Year	Cash flows £s	
	A	B
0	(9,000)	(9,000)
1	1,000	7,000
2	2,000	3,000
3	8,000	1,000
4	5,000	1,000
NPV	2,984	1,275

However, if near cash flows are valued more than distant ones, B has its attractions. If we calculate the time taken to recover the capital outlay in each case, A has a *payback period* of 2¾ years and B 1¾ years, therefore B, with a quicker turnround of capital, is the more attractive.

Certainly, as regards new products, new technology, early product obsolescence, and unstable economic or political regimes, early payback of capital looms large in investors' minds. 'A bird in the hand is worth two in the bush' as the saying goes.

Immediately prior to the British/Chinese agreement regarding the political future of Hong Kong for example, early payback was reported to be the prime evaluation criterion applied to property investment. Research indicates that payback is the most used approach, very often in conjunction with NPV.

Payback, by definition, ignores profitability, i.e. cash flows after payback, and consequently can cause suboptimal decisions if used in isolation. It could be used to 'screen out' projects with painfully long payback periods or when profitability between alternatives shows marginal differences. Otherwise the 'risk quality' of cash flows beyond the capital break-even point ought to be assessed – however subjectively – in making the final decision. By itself, payback does not satisfactorily quantify the level of uncertainty in a project.

Risk-adjusted discount rates

In the illustrations used in this book so far, a rate of 10% has been applied as the rate appropriate to the risk inherent in each project.

If you invest in government bonds, the return is guaranteed. A 12% security will pay just that and investors in that security are presumed to be quite happy with that yield. In comparison, a much higher return would be expected from a company selling fashionable clothes – perhaps as much as 18%. The reason is, that although there is a possibility that returns will at times be much higher than 18%, they are just as likely to be lower than that. Indeed, the risk of loss may be quite high and it is this risk that forces up the investor's required rate of return.

Businesses tend to have a mixture of investment projects, some more risky than others, and although the investor demands a single rate of return, it represents a weighted average of the rates appropriate to the risks of all the projects. It follows that a business must estimate and apply the risk rate applicable to each project, otherwise there is a danger that it will make suboptimal investment decisions.

Supposing a company's overall required investment rate is 15%. An investment of £50,000 is proposed which is forecast to produce a net cash inflow in each of the next three years of £23,000, and to require a rate of return of 20%. The comparative NPVs at 15% and 20% are summarized below:

Year	Cash flow	15% DCF factors	Net Cash flow £	20% DCF factors	Net Cash flow £
0	(50,000)	1.000	(50,000)	1.000	(50,000)
1	23,000	.870	20,010	.833	19,159
2	23,000	.756	17,388	.694	15,962
3	23,000	.658	15,134	.579	13,317
Net present value			2,532		(1,562)

At the company's average rate of return of 15% the project is acceptable with a positive NPV of £2,532. When a more appropriate risk rate of 20% is applied, however, we have a negative NPV and an unacceptable project.

Best/worst possible outcomes

Although payback and risk-adjusted discount rates have their uses, their main weakness is that they are applied to one discrete set of cash flows. Depending upon the forecast economic conditions, the actual cash flows could range from high to low in between boom and slump respectively, and one way to portray this is to estimate the cash flow that would result if everything went wrong, and the expected cash flow if everything went right. We would then be setting lower and upper limits to probable cash flows. If the lower limit is profitable, no further analysis is required; but if not, a forecast of the most likely outcome should be produced.

For relatively low-value projects, this high/low/most likely analysis may provide sufficient indication of the range of possible outcomes, but it does not specify the probability of each possible state occurring.

For example, a project may be forecast to produce a negative NPV of £10,000 at worst, but a positive best outcome of £30,000. Knowledge of how likely the best and worst are to happen, would give the appraiser a more helpful backcloth against which to make his decision. For this we need some analysis of probability.

Probability analysis

If each of the three-point estimates discussed in the previous section, together with other possible outcomes, were given a decimal rating of between zero (i.e. nil likelihood), and 1 (absolute certainty) according to their estimated likelihood of occurring, with the rankings totalling 1, the resulting probability distribution could be very enlightening.

The data might be as follows:

	Project A	
Probability(1)	Outcome(2)	Weighted value(1 × 2)
	£	£
0.10	6,000	600
0.15	8,000	1,200
0.35	12,000	4,200
0.25	15,000	3,750
0.15	20,000	3,000
Expected	value	12,750

£12,000 is shown as the most likely outcome, but other values could occur. The expected value, which is the weighted average of all the possible outcomes, represents the amount that would be realized, on the average, if this project were repeated many times.

Now let us look at the probability distribution of another project, B:

Probability(1)	Project B Outcome(2) £	Weighted value (1 × 2) £
0.05	(5,000)	(250)
0.10	15,000	1,500
0.70	20,000	14,000
0.10	25,000	2,500
0.05	30,000	1,500
Expected value		19,250

Note the high probability of attaining £20,000, with other, widely dispersed values possible, but not greatly so.

The dispersion of possible outcomes around the expected value of £19,250, can be measured statistically by calculating the *standard deviation*, and this can be useful in further analysis. For most purposes, however, a distribution of possible outcomes is informative enough.

The weakness of project B is that it reveals a possible loss of £5,000. It appears better than A overall, but if management is highly sensitive to risk, e.g. because existing operations are doing badly, they might not want to chance the risk of any loss.

Another way of making use of probability distributions is to calculate the cumulative probability of attaining certain values. For example, there is a 75% chance of obtaining at least £12,000 from Project A.

Probability factors might be based upon past experience of similar projects, or might have to be subjectively estimated. Whichever method is used, investment managers are disciplined to consider future outcomes and this ought to result in better decisions.

Sensitivity analysis

A more objective way of assessing risk is to analyse the effect on a project of possible changes in any one of its variables, such as capital cost, sales volume, price, foreign currency exchange rates, operating costs, rate of return and life expectancy.

Holding other aspects constant, we can ask how much change can take place in any one variable and still leave the project just viable, i.e. NPV would equal zero.

Example:
It is proposed to market a new product at a selling price of £10, having a variable cost of £6.50 per unit. Sales of 2,000 units per annum for five years are expected, and the initial capital cost will be £20,000. The required rate of return is 15%.

The NPV of the new product proposal is calculated as follows:

3.50×2000

$(£7,000 \times 3.353) - 20,000 = £3,471$

\ sum of PV factors for yrs 1-5 incl.

showing the proposal to be profitable – yielding a positive NPV of £3,471. But how sensitive are each of the factors to change?

If capital cost is examined, it can be seen that its cost can increase by the NPV of the project, i.e. if its capital cost was £23,471 the project would just break even at zero NPV.

Other variables can be tested in a similar way and a summary of the maximum changes is given below:

Life of project – reduce to 4 years	20% reduction
Rate of return – increase to 22½%	50% increase
Net cash flow – reduce to £5,966	15% reduction
Sales price – reduce by £0.517 a unit	5% reduction
Variable cost – increase by £0.517 a unit	8% increase
Sales volume – reduce to 1,705 units	15% reduction

Note that variable costs and sales price are the most sensitive, should therefore be closely vetted before the project starts, and then on a continuing basis. They are the factors that put the project most at risk.

It might be unrealistic to probe the effects of change on single variables as there may be interdependencies. For example, if operating costs increase, sales price might be adjusted automtically. If capital cost increased, perhaps to improve technology, operating costs would be affected. Sales price changes could affect demand.

This additional complication in analysis, together with associated uncertainties, will obviously be a daunting task, but can now be made easier by microcomputer packaged programs. The 'what if' questioning facility of computers makes for more informed decisions.

Whatever the sophistication of analysis, the results can only be as good as the inputs permit and it is the latter that should receive most attention. In addition, the investor should weigh carefully the effect of a new project on his existing portfolio. Even if an investment promises an exciting return, it may not be an attractive addition to a portfolio already bulging with risky projects of a similar nature.

6 Resource Flow Control

INTRODUCTION

The activities of a business during a financial year combine investment projects in progress with new projects commencing and others terminating within the year. It would appear reasonable to presume, therefore, that business financial reports are presented in the cash-flow mode used to appraise investments, to facilitate comparison of actual with planned cash flows.

Some businesses do make such comparisons as part of their retrospective monitoring of investment decisions, but there is no obligation to do so. Cash-flow accounting, as it is called, has its supporters, but its introduction is frustrated by statutory and non-statutory regulations.

The Companies Act requires limited companies to produce profit and loss accounts and balance sheets in prescribed form. The Inland Revenue assumes that taxable profit has been computed by applying recognized accounting principles. The Accounting Standards Committee recommends the application of standard practices in the measurement of profit and portrayal of a company's financial position in its balance sheet. More compellingly, profit and loss reporting is compatible with the investors' objective of stable and growing dividends, payable out of equally stable and growing earnings.

As outlined in Chapter 3 (Figure 4) profit is measured conventionally by setting against the sales revenue for a period the costs expired in earning that revenue. That is, sales are *matched* against their relevant costs. Profit is therefore more evenly reported than it would be if all cash receipts and payments, capital and revenue, were fully reflected in the accounts of the period in which they are received and paid.

The management accountant also adopts the *matching principle* when preparing control information in both actual and budgeted form, and also to ascertain full product cost as a starting point for setting selling prices (see Chapter 11).

This chapter outlines the systems and methods used to control the flow of resources through production and service cost centres, for their eventual inclusion in product and period costs.

MATERIAL CONTROL

The chairman of a British group of companies recently stated that any fool can sell – it is buying at the right price that is more critical to the achievement of a satisfactory return on capital employed. Buying price is important of course, but buying the right materials, in the most economic quantities, at the right time, are equally important if production targets are to be achieved and investment in inventories is to be minimized.

What to order

This is governed by product specifications, but an efficient buyer will always have his ear to the ground to discover new and substitute materials and components of advantageous quality and price. Other economies can be realized by reducing the variety of materials purchased by *standardization*, e.g. reducing the variety of colours of paint stocked, or by introducing value analysis into the decision process.

Value analysis is a formalized technique involving a rigorous analysis of products at the design stage or at any time during their saleable lives, to determine their value characteristics. These are the attributes that a customer looks for in a product and include its use value (functional qualities), appeal value (colour, style, etc.) and second-hand value (e.g. trade-in price). The object of value analysis is to build into the product the optimum of desired value at minimum cost, by introducing the most up-to-date designs, materials and methods of manufacture. No more value need be built into the product than is desired by the customer. For example, moulded plastic bumper bars are now fitted to many cars, because they are cheaper and equally as functional as chromium-plated steel ones.

How much to order

Supposing the estimated annual usage of a component by Hemming Agricultural Machinery Ltd is 20,000 units. Usage is even throughout the year and only one order per annum is placed with the supplier. Because only one delivery is made, average stock will be high, i.e. $20,000 \div 2 = 10,000$, and consequently stockholding costs will be very high. On the other hand, the costs of ordering will be negligible. If two orders are placed there will be less in stock (i.e. average 5,000), which will reduce holding costs, but ordering costs will increase. Thus, the higher the number of orders placed, the lower are stockholding costs, but the higher are ordering costs.

Stockholding costs include interest on the capital invested in stocks, storage, insurance, rates, security, building maintenance, heating, etc. Ordering costs include buying-department staff costs, receiving and handling.

Assuming that the cost of each Hemming component is £10, that holding cost is 10% of stock value and the cost of placing an order is £1, the total annual cost of stockholding and ordering when different numbers of orders are placed, is as follows:

No. of orders	4	20	50	100	200	400
Size of order	5,000	1,000	400	200	100	50
Average stock (50% order)	2,500	500	200	100	50	25
Holding cost	£2,500	£500	£200	£100	£50	£25
Ordering cost (£1 per order)	£4	£20	£50	£100	£200	£400
Total annual cost	£2,504	£520	£250	£200	£250	£425

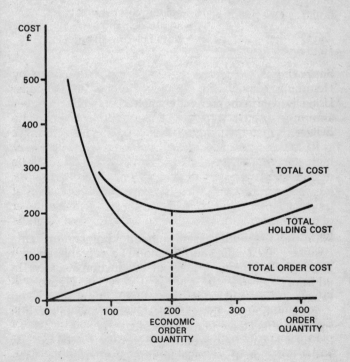

Figure 5. Economic order quantity

Placing 100 orders a year results in the lowest total of ordering and holding cost of £200, therefore the economic order quantity is 200 units.

The same information is graphed in Figure 5 above, showing that the *economic order quantity* (EOQ) is at the point where ordering and holding costs are equal, and total £200.

As costs of ordering and holding stock are equal at the EOQ point, we can build a simple mathematical model to solve the problem, as follows:

$$\frac{Q}{2} \times H = \frac{A \times P}{Q}$$

where Q = EOQ
H = holding cost per unit
A = annual demand
P = cost of placing an order

$$\text{and } Q^2 = \frac{2AP}{H}$$

$$\text{finally } Q = \sqrt{\frac{2AP}{H}}$$

Using the data in the previous example:

$$EOQ = \sqrt{\frac{2 \times 20{,}000 \times 1}{1}}$$

$$= \sqrt{40{,}000}$$

$$= \underline{200}$$

Although the model assumes that holding and ordering costs are fixed, this simplification is acceptable given a relatively unchanging level of production activity. In addition, because the total cost curve in Figure 5 is relatively flat either side of the EOQ, minor errors and approximations in the variables used in the calculation may not affect the end result significantly.

Practical constraints on the use of the model include restrictions on the available storage space, the availability of quantity discounts (though the model can be modified in this respect), the seasonal nature of supplies, the shelf-life of products and delivery schedules imposed by suppliers.

When to order

If deliveries from suppliers normally take two weeks to arrive, then replenishment orders should be placed with them when the level of stocks represents two weeks' supply. For example, if usage is 200 units a week, an order (the EOQ) will be placed when the stock level falls to 400 units. Figure 6(a) illustrates that, with *certain* knowledge of usage and lead time, delivery takes place just as stock is exhausted.

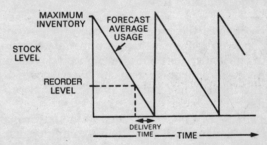

Figure 6(a) Stock levels when usage and replenishment times are known

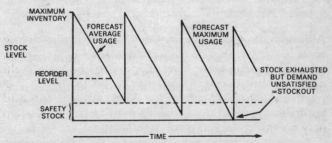

Figure 6(b). Stock levels when usage and replenishment are uncertain

Lead times and usage may not be stable and provision against running out of stock then becomes necessary (see Figure 6(b)). *Safety stocks* have a cost, however, and this has to be balanced against the cost of running out of stock. 'Stock outs' may cause loss of customers and the probability of this happening at various levels of safety stock must be estimated. The point at which the cost of carrying safety stocks plus the cost of 'stock outs' is lowest, indicates the safety stock level. Notice that uncertainty causes the reorder level to be at a higher level to include the required safety stock.

Controlling material flow

Figure 7 outlines the progressive stages in purchasing, issuing and recording materials in a manufacturing concern. An efficient system of documenting and recording is vitally necessary, not only for accounting purposes, but to ensure that the right materials arrive at the right place at the right time.

The *purchase requisition* submitted to the buyer may be triggered automatically if the system is computerized, by a message from the stores ledger that the reorder level has been reached. Other requests to purchase may be raised by the production planning department for new product materials not yet carried in stock, and also by any departmental head for supplies and equipment of any kind.

The buyer, ideally after making *enquiries* of several suppliers, sends a *purchase order*, and eventually the material is received, checked by the good-inwards department as to quality and quantity, and is detailed on a *goods-received note* (GRN). One copy of the GRN goes to the buyer to write off the outstanding order record; one to the accounts department for checking against the order and invoice – the latter authorising payment to the supplier; and one to the stores department with the materials.

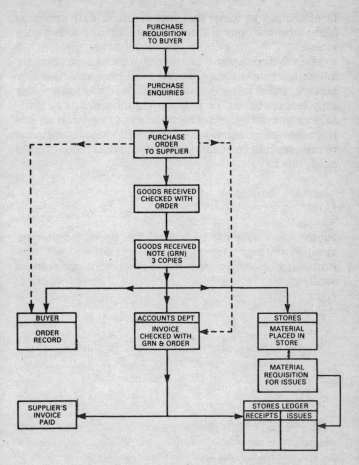

Figure 7 Procedure for material acquisition, recording and issue

A *stores record* is maintained into which the quantity and value of materials received is entered. Issues of materials to production are made by authorized materials requisitions which are also entered into the stores ledger to keep that record up to date continuously, and also into the appropriate job or process cost record.

As already indicated, all the above procedures may be integrated into a computerized stock record which can provide information at the press of a button to the storekeeper, buyer, production planner, financial manager or any other person authorized to key into it. For example, information on slow-moving stock items can be obtained automatically and without delay.

Material storage

Sophisticated mathematical models to control economic buying, and systems to control the flow of materials may all be for nought if the obvious – efficient storekeeping – is ignored. Good practice in this respect implies:

- the employment of a well-trained stores staff
- use of the most efficient equipment – for storage and handling
- easy access to items – stored in logical order
- siting of stores convenient to users
- security against theft and fire
- protection against deterioration
- a system of continuously checking physical with recorded stocks.

LABOUR CONTROL

How much labour?

Labour is a considerable proportion of total cost of production, despite mechanization and automation, and therefore warrants tight control. Labour requirements depend upon product specifications and manufacturing operations, but labour efficiency and limiting factors restricting the availability of labour must also be considered.

Should there be a shortage of skilled labour in a department then, in the short term, either total output will have to be reduced to accommodate this limitation, or overtime working, subcontracting or some other remedy, adopted. In the long term, a training scheme may solve the problem or a change in production method, such as automation.

In continuous processing operations, e.g. food manufacturing, or where there is a high degree of automation or mechanization, labour takes on the role of machine minding. In these conditions, labour is a fixed cost, rather than varying with output.

Another factor to take account of in determining labour requirement is the *'learning curve'*. 'Practice makes perfect' – eventually; but in the meantime, the time taken to complete new tasks may be high, and with

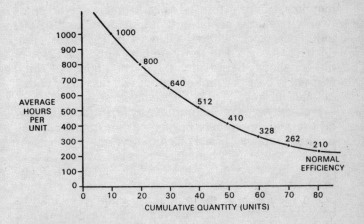

Figure 8. Learning curve

it the cost of labour. Increasing familiarity with a job over time, reduces the average time taken per unit. Figure 8 shows that improvements in efficiency are high initially, then progressively reduce, until a plateau of normal efficiency is reached.

Figure 8 adopts an 80% efficiency factor, i.e. each doubling of output reduces the average time per unit to 80% of the previous average time, which is quite a common phenomenon. Learning curve analysis is particularly applicable to operations requiring skill, e.g. aircraft manufacture or underwater maintenance of oil rigs, but will also be in evidence when labour turnover is high, and with it, learning costs.

Labour productivity

Productivity is the relationship between output and the number of workers or available working hours. For example, the productivity of ten workers who each work forty hours a week and produce 10,000 units in that time, can be expressed as 1,000 units per worker, or twenty-five units per hour. If output increases to 12,000 units per week without changes in resources, productivity has risen to thirty units per hour or 120% of the previous figure. In these conditions of high efficiency, cost per unit of output will decrease, with a possible improvement in competitiveness.

Productivity may also improve by (a) introducing new or improved machinery or methods, or (b) introducing incentive schemes based on efficiency.

The costs and benefits of each of the above approaches needs to be carefully analysed. New machinery or methods may be costly, and the consequent reduction in the number of employees may be offset to some extent by high redundancy payments and higher wages agreed to be paid to the remaining workers. Output per hour might increase, but is not beneficial if costs increase proportionately.

Incentive schemes

These are arrangements for paying workers above their normal rates of pay for beating a specified target of output in an agreed length of time.

To be acceptable to both employer and employee an incentive scheme should meet at least the following conditions:

- it should be easy to understand and to administer
- targets of efficiency should be attainable, otherwise the scheme will fall into disrepute
- complaints and disputes must be settled promptly
- the scheme must be compatible with conditions, e.g. a goal of improved quality may not be realized if linked with an incentive scheme calling for high output
- there should be few production hold-ups, and allowances must be made for unavoidable delays
- prior discussions should be held by all interested parties to iron out difficulties before the scheme is introduced
- the scheme should be of benefit to both employer and employee.

There are many variations of incentive scheme but most of them fall into one of four classes:

- higher day-rate schemes
- piecework plans
- individual bonus schemes
- group bonus schemes.

Higher day rate

In these schemes the worker is offered a higher than normal rate of pay in return for an agreed minimum (but attainable) level of productivity. Efficient supervision is essential, and anyone unable to meet the set target should receive additional training.

Example:

Workers are currently filling 100 boxes per hour and are paid £5 per hour. They are offered £5.50 per hour in return for a minimum total factory efficiency of 120%.

Comparative costs per box are:

$$before: \frac{500}{100} = 5p. \quad after: \frac{550}{120} = 4.58p.$$

which benefits the employer by reducing labour cost per box, and the employee by 50p. per hour.

Even if the minimum efficiency level were to be agreed at 110% and result in an unchanged labour cost, i.e. 550/110 = 5p. per box, the employer could still benefit by a reduction in fixed overhead cost per box.

Piecework plans

These reward individual effort more effectively than high day-rate schemes, as payment is made for each unit produced. The more efficient the worker the more he earns. Differentiated (higher) rates are sometimes paid to spur on employees to greater effort, e.g. 10p. each for the first 200 units, 11p. for the next 100 units and so on. Piecework is best suited to output of similar articles to enable the worker to overcome the 'learning effect'.

A guaranteed minimum wage is normally paid when production is low for reasons beyond the control of the worker.

The drawbacks of such plans are the possible increase in volume of shoddy work and the high cost of administration.

Individual bonus schemes

Most of these schemes require a standard allowed time to be determined for each job. Payment at normal hourly rate is paid for the actual time taken, plus a bonus based upon the difference between time allowed and time taken. For example, the Halsey scheme provides for a bonus of 50% of the time saved, paid at normal day rate. Thus, a job with a time allowed of ten hours, completed in six hours, with an hourly rate of £4, would pay $6 + .5(10-6) \times 4 = £32$.

Though such schemes may improve productivity and therefore unit cost, they are usually resented because the benefits of the time saved are shared between employer and employee. In addition, the cost of administering them is relatively high and the least efficient workers are not sufficiently encouraged to improve their performance.

Consequently, a system known as 'measured day work' is more frequently met in industry today. Standard times for each job are set by scientific measurement and payment is made at an increasing rate per hour, based upon the efficiency attained by each worker during the period just ended.

Example:
If the total of all the allowed times for jobs completed by an employee during a four-weekly period was 120 hours, and the total time taken was 100 hours, his efficiency would be $120/100 \times 100\% = 120\%$. Reference to an agreed table of differential pay rates for progressively higher levels of efficiency is then made (see below) and the worker would be paid at £4.50 per hour

for hours worked during the following four-weekly period.

Efficiency %	Rate per hour
£	£
up to 90	3.00
95	3.20
100	3.40
110	4.00
120	4.50
125	5.00

Group incentive schemes

Where work is completed by teams of employees and individual performance is hard to measure, a bonus based upon the output of the team is more appropriate. Car manufacture and road building attract this type of scheme. The bonus may still be founded on one of the schemes already discussed, i.e. piecework, measured day work, or high day-rate, the difference being that the bonus is pooled for sharing. Sharing the bonus is a sensitive matter and it is probably best left to the employees to decide this issue. Supervisors and indirect workers, being members of the team, can be included in the bonus share-out.

The advantages of group schemes are that they are administratively easier and cheaper, they encourage flexible working by employees, and slower workers are encouraged to greater effort as part of a team. The main disadvantage is that more efficient workers may be penalized by having to work at the pace of the slowest member of the team.

Labour-control system

Efficient manpower planning and the search for higher productivity are vital to labour cost control; but it is also important to ensure that the available labour is fully accounted for.

Figure 9 shows the basic stages of a typical system for recording labour, the following being a brief explanation of the procedure at each stage.

1 *Attendance time* – starting and finishing times are usually recorded by workers on clock cards at the entrance to their place of work. Absenteeism and lateness are disclosed at this point.

2 *Job instructions* – issued to workers by production planning, together with requisitions to draw materials from stores, and job cards or time sheets to record the time taken to complete each task.

3 *Job times recorded* – by clock at the work place or on a time sheet covering the whole week. Idle time, e.g. waiting for instructions, is recorded separately and analysed to show the reasons for non-productive time.

4 *Reconciling attendance with work time* – the total clocked hours for the week should equal recorded productive plus non-productive time, accounted for as in 3 above.

5 *Job labour costs computed* – and summarized, including bonuses.

6 *Wages calculated* – for each employee the total gross pay on the job-card summary is entered into the weekly payroll; deductions are made for taxation, NHI, pension, etc., to give the net pay due to each employee.

7 *Wages paid* – cash is obtained from the bank for the total net pay shown on the payroll; cash and pay slips are put into packets for employees.

8 *Job cost records* – gross pay relevant to individual jobs is entered on individual job-cost records from the job-card summary (see 5 above).

9 *Total wages* – entered into the main accounting system: debits to individual cost-centre control accounts, and credits to cash and deduction accounts.

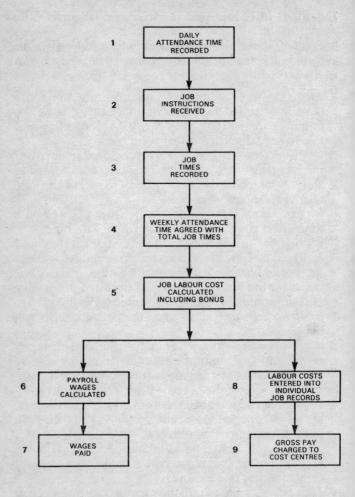

Figure 9. Stages in a labour recording system

Labour-control reports

Periodic reports to management will enable them to keep their fingers on the pulse of operating activity. The two main reasons for activity not being as planned are: (a) *the efficiency* of workers was higher or lower than expected, and (b) *capacity* (hours available) were more or less than planned.

Supposing total planned hours in a year were 200,000, but that only 180,000 hours were actually worked; during which time output equivalent to 160,000 hours was produced.

Efficiency is measured by relating actual output (160,000 hours) to actual hours worked (180,000); whilst capacity working is calculated by relating actual hours worked to planned hours, as follows:

$$\underline{\text{Efficiency}} \times \underline{\text{Capacity}} = \underline{\text{Activity}}$$

$$\frac{160,000}{180,000} \times \frac{180,000}{200,000} = \frac{160,000}{200,000}$$

$$89\% \quad \times \quad 90\% \quad = \quad 80\%$$

The activity performance of 80% has been caused by fewer operating hours being available (90%), and the inefficient use of those hours (89%).

Reports covering this poor performance should cover:

1 *Lost production time* – perhaps due to waiting for instructions or materials.
2 *Overtime* – indicating possible reasons for jobs taking longer than planned.
3 *Labour turnover* – relating the total number of employees leaving during a period to the average number employed during that period. A high percentage turnover affects both capacity and efficiency as time is lost in training new employees and in the

'learning curve'. Reasons for employees leaving should be investigated and appropriate action taken to reduce the rate of labour turnover.

4 *Lateness/absenteeism* – will explain lost production time. Workers may respond to some form of attendance bonus, but if not, dismissal might be the only way to deal with the problem – depending, of course, on the availability of replacement labour.

5 *Extra time allowance* – e.g. for non-standard material causing delay, might be the reason for lost capacity.

OVERHEAD CONTROL

Indirect material, labour and expenses are generally referred to as overheads, and you will recall that they represent those costs that are not wholly or readily identifiable with one particular product or process. However, manufacturing overheads are part of the cost of production and have to be charged to the cost of each product in the most equitable way. Other, non-manufacturing overheads, of selling, distribution and administration, are period costs and are written off against revenue in the period in which they are incurred.

Overheads are a significant proportion of total costs in any organization, their label of 'indirect' sometimes being interpreted as 'uncontrollable'. Spending on overheads comes out of the same pool of financial resources as direct costs and must therefore be justified. We will be dealing with the question of justification in later chapters on budgetary control.

In this section we describe a system of classifying, allocating and apportioning overheads:

a to facilitate cost-centre expenditure control, and

b to charge a reasonable proportion of overheads to each job or process for purposes of stock valuation to aid profit measurement, pricing and other decisions.

Classifying overheads

Indirect materials include such items as tools, nuts, bolts, glue, lubricating oil, cleaning rags, office stationery, heating oil, etc.

Indirect labour is classified according to the service rendered, e.g. management, supervisory, clerical, quality control, storekeeping, idle time, overtime premium, security, salesmen, etc.

Indirect expenses are any costs not classified as indirect materials or labour, e.g. gas, water, rates, employers' NHI, depreciation, repairs to machinery, employees' restaurant subsidy, postages, consultancy fees, transport, etc.

Most businesses have an accounts coding system and each type of expense is allotted a unique code to enable it to be identified by the data processing system and entered into the appropriate account. For example, each expense head could be given a three-digit number: tools – 123; stationery – 128; heating oil – 143.

Allocation and apportionment of overheads

The next stage is to collect costs into cost centres to enable control to be exercised by responsible supervisors.

Cost centres are normally created for each of the production and production service departments, and for the selling, distribution and administration functions.

For this purpose each cost centre could be allotted a two-digit code. For example, the machine maintenance department might be code 14; any tools expense incurred by that department would then be coded 14123 (see above for expense codes), the first two digits indicating the cost centre and the last three the expense classification. The data processing system then searches and finds the relevant expense record and account 14123 is charged accordingly.

Two basic rules apply in charging expenses to cost centres:

- if a cost is incurred by a specific cost centre ALLOCATE it to that centre; such an item (a supervisor's salary for example) is a direct cost of that centre, identifiable with only one department
- if a cost is incurred for the benefit of two or more cost centres, such as rent and rates APPORTION it between the centres.

Expenses directly allocable to a cost centre, such as maintenance tools, are easily dealt with, but apportionment can be a problem because a reasonable basis for sharing has to be decided. Not all overheads are directly proportionate to volume of output or of goods sold. Some costs are fixed, such as rents, rates, heating and lighting; others relate to value of assets, such as depreciation and insurance; whilst some relate to the number of employees, e.g. personnel costs. The question to ask is: what primary influence causes each cost to be incurred? This question is dealt with in detail in Chapter 8, but for the purposes of this chapter some common bases for apportioning costs are summarized below:

Basis	Cost
Floor area of buildings	occupancy costs, e.g. rent, rates, security
Volume of buildings	heating
Number of employees	restaurant subsidy
Value	depreciation, insurance
Labour hours worked	works manager's salary and expenses
Technical estimates	electric power, water, gas – when not metered

NOTE:

Technical estimates are based on the rating, size or capacity of the consuming unit, e.g. the power estimated to be used per hour by an electric motor depends upon its consumption rating.

Charging service centre costs to production centres

Ultimately, each job or product must be assigned a measured amount of production overheads and this can only be achieved if all service department costs are absorbed into production centres. Service departments are those that play a supporting role to the main operating activity.

For example, hospital wards and operating theatres cannot function without the services of laundry, kitchen, radiography, physiotherapy, maintenance and cleaning.

Manufacturing companies require personnel specialists, works administrators, machine and building maintenance technicians, and production planners to support the departments directly engaged in producing goods.

Summarizing overheads by cost centre is useful for control purposes, but another objective is to assign a measured amount of manufacturing overhead to each job or product. As production operations are only completed in production departments, we have therefore to transfer service department overheads to production departments.

This can be effected by invoking the same two rules that we apply when charging overhead to cost centres, i.e. direct allocation and logical apportionment. For example, a separate cost record is sometimes made for each maintenance job completed, and can therefore be charged on a direct allocation basis to the department for whom the work has been done. Other service costs will be apportioned using bases that represent the most likely causal relationship between the costs and user departments.

Common bases of apportionment include:

Basis	Service
Labour hours worked	production planning; work study
Machine hours worked	machine maintenance
Number of employees	personnel
Floor area	all occupancy costs
Number of stores requisitions	stores
Technical estimate	steam; power; compressed air

Figure 10, below, summarizes the main steps in the classification, allocation and apportionment of overheads to the cost centres and products described above.

To further clarify the process of overhead absorption a worked example is given below.

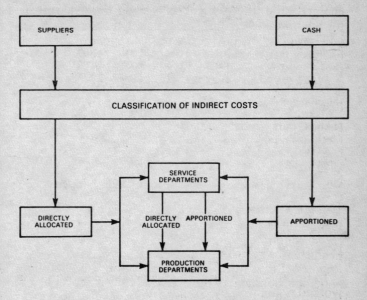

Figure 10. Steps in charging overheads to production departments

	Works admin.	Stores	Maint.	Machining	Assembly
Costs directly allocated	£2,000	£5,000	£10,000	£40,000	£30,000
Floor area (sq. ft)	400	6,600	3,000	20,000	10,000
No of employees	10	30	60	300	600
Machine value			£50,000	£400,000	£50,000
Labour hours worked		50,000	50,000	100,000	300,000
Machine hours worked				300,000	100,000
No of stores requisitions			5,000	20,000	25,000

Note: Works admin. = works administration. Maint. = maintenance.

Costs to be apportioned:	£
Rent and rates	20,000
Canteen loss	10,000
Depreciation of machines	15,000

Required: Draw up a schedule showing the allocation and apportionment of the overheads given above, using the most appropriate basis from those detailed above.

Schedule of overhead distribution

	Works	Stores	Maint.	Machining	Assembly
	£	£	£	£	£
Directly allocated	2,000	5,000	10,000	40,000	30,000
Rent and rates (area)	200	3,300	1,500	10,000	5,000
Canteen loss (employees)	100	300	600	3,000	6,000
Depreciation (value of machines)			1,500	12,000	1,500
	2,300	8,600	13,600	65,000	42,500
Works admin. (labour hours worked)	(2,300)	230	230	460	1,380
Stores (requisitions)		(8,830)	883	3,532	4,415
Maintenance (machine hours)			(14,713)	11,035	3,678
				£80,027	£51,973

The overheads are distributed in two stages:

1 allocation and apportionment of expenses to all cost centres
2 apportionment of service department overheads to production cost centres.

The process is completed by apportioning to jobs completed, but this is dealt with in Chapter 7.

7   Ascertaining Cost Per Unit

Identifying the unit of output

Building contractors, civil engineers and shipbuilders
work on jobs or contracts, each of which is unique and
can be separately identified. In other industries, a single
product, such as coal, steel or cement, is processed and
output is measured in tons. Some manufacturing firms
produce a range of products through a sequence of
processes, including food, beer, paint and cosmetics,
which might be measured in numbers of cans, gallons,
litres and batches of 100,000, respectively.

Service industries have their own output measurements. Hotels deal in bed nights, hospitals in patient
days, electricity distribution in kilowatt hours, and
transport in passenger miles.

The type of operation, therefore, establishes the unit
used as the measure of activity, in respect of which,
costs can be meaningfully ascertained.

Necessity and relevance of unit cost

The cost of a job or other unit of output is needed for
various purposes:

- to prepare a cost estimate for quoting or for fixing a
  selling price
- to ascertain actual cost to compare with estimated
  or budgeted cost
- to value finished or part-finished work for stock
  valuation

■ to ascertain the profitability of a job, product or service.

The relevant cost to apply to each of the above will vary according to purpose.

Under full-capacity working in the long term, full product and period costs will normally be used to help determine selling prices, but in the short term, perhaps when the order book is low, less than full cost might be used.

All product and period costs will again be used when comparing actual with planned costs, but for stock valuation only product cost applies.

Measurement of profit must finally take account of all costs, but by deducting only variable costs from selling price we can see how much each product contributes towards fixed costs and profit.

Three basic types of costing

When it is necessary to ascertain the cost of each customer's order or contract, or the cost of a particular batch of production, *job costing* is used. This simply means that a separate record is created on which is accumulated the costs of each job. This record is additional to the usual accounting records.

Where like units are produced through a continuous sequence of operations a system of *process costing* applies. As units proceed through successive processes, the costs of each process during a particular period are divided by the output for that period to give the cost per unit at each stage. The finished output of one process becomes the input of the next, together with its costs to date, until the end of the production cycle, when the final accumulated cost per unit is ascertained.

Operating costing is used in service industries, when the cost per unit of service is determined in the same way as process costing, i.e. by dividing total costs by total units of service output.

Job cost

The direct costs of a job are relatively easy to identify. Direct materials are transferred from stores to each job, evidenced by a *stores requisition*; direct labour is specifically identified with each job on separate *job tickets*; and other direct expenses are job coded when received from the supplier.

Indirect costs, by definition, cannot be directly related to particular jobs or products. Therefore, after they have been classified, allocated and apportioned into production cost centres, as shown in Chapter 6, some method of averaging has to be adopted to assign them to jobs or products.

The obvious approach would be to total each month's overhead costs and divide them by the number of units produced in that month.

Supposing a manufacturer incurs costs as follows:

Direct materials   £6 per unit
Direct labour   £5 per unit
Indirect costs   fixed per month £1,000, variable £2 per unit

During March, building repairs cost £400, this being additional to the costs given above.

Output of units for the months of March, April and May, were 400, 500 and 1,000 respectively.

A schedule summarizing the cost per unit for each month is given below:

	March	April	May
Fixed costs	1,000	1,000	1,000
Building repairs	400		
	1,400	1,000	1,000
Output (units)	400	500	1,000
Fixed cost per unit	£3.50	2.00	1.00
Direct materials	6.00	6.00	6.00
Direct labour	5.00	5.00	5.00
Variable overhead	2.00	2.00	2.00
Total cost per unit	£16.50	15.00	14.00

What cost should we use when charging a customer – particularly the same customer – in March, April and May? He would be puzzled if his jobs cost different prices in each month and he would not be billed until after the month end because cost would not be available until then.

Suppose some of the units delivered to a customer in May were processed differently from other units, perhaps requiring more machine time than normal. Would we still charge £14 per unit? These questions emphasize the problems associated with unit cost ascertainment, which can be summarized:

- output may vary from period to period whilst a large proportion of indirect costs (i.e. fixed) remain the same, causing fluctuations in cost per unit
- overhead costs may vary seasonally or because of infrequent, spasmodic expenditure, causing fluctuations in costs at variance with output
- using period-end cost rates causes customer invoicing to be delayed
- products may require different processing and therefore not cost the same to produce.

The first three problems can be overcome by using *predetermined overhead cost rates*, calculated by estimating the total overhead costs for the year ahead and dividing that cost by the estimated production for the same period. For example, if estimated overhead cost is £10,000 and estimated output 1,000 units, the overhead rate to apply for the whole year would be £10.

The fourth problem can be dealt with by calculating different predetermined overhead cost rates for each production department, expressed as a rate per machine or labour hour.

For example, using the figures of overhead summarized by production departments at the end of Chapter 6, and assuming that these are budgeted costs and output for the coming year, predetermined overhead rates can be calculated as follows:

	Machining	Assembly	Total
Total overhead	£80,027	£51,973	£132,000
Labour hours	100,000	300,000	400,000
Labour hour rate	£0.80027	£0.17324	£0.33

Applying the above overhead rates, we can calculate the production cost whose direct material cost is £649, and direct labour £4000. Hours worked in the machining and assembly departments were 700 and 200 respectively.

Cost of Job 789	
Direct material	649
Direct labour	4,000
Overhead:	
machining 700 × .80027	560
assembly 200 × .17324	35
Total production cost	£5,244

Note that, had the total factory overhead rate of £0.33 been used, the overhead charge would have been 900 × £0.33 = £297, which is considerably less than the charge based on the separate departmental rates. When jobs require different production operations, which incur significantly different overhead costs, the application of departmental overhead rates will give a more equitable apportionment of cost to jobs than an overall factory rate. In addition, the predetermination of the rates ensures a consistent application of cost throughout the year and customers can be invoiced without delay. For stock valuation purposes, incomplete jobs at a period end are valued at accumulated direct costs, plus overhead absorbed up to that time.

Given that total overhead and production are as forecast, all overhead will be absorbed by the end of the year. This is unlikely to happen however, and any over- or under-absorbed overhead remaining at year end is written off to cost of sales.

For selling-price purposes we also have to add a proportionate part of selling and administration overheads. Practice in this respect varies, but a widely used approach is to predetermine a rate by expressing forecast selling and administration cost as a percentage of forecast production cost. If we suppose that this rate is 15% and add a further 25% of total cost as profit, the charge to the customer for Job 789 would be:

Selling price make-up Job 789

	£
Total production cost	5,244
Add selling and admin. × 15%	787
Total cost	6,031
Add profit × 25%	1,508
Selling price	£7,539

Contract cost

Contract costing follows the same principles as job costing because the work involved on each customer order is unique, but has additional characteristics arising out of the high value and relatively long lead time of each contract. Contract costing is applicable to the construction of houses, office blocks, tunnels, bridges, roads, harbours and ships.

Cost records are maintained for each contract, which carries its own labour force of direct and indirect workers, and has services supplied on-site. A high proportion of the costs of each contract are therefore direct, the major indirect cost being a proportion of head office costs, perhaps charged to each contract as a percentage of total direct costs. Plant and vehicles are a conspicuous item in contract work, and are normally charged directly to a contract when assigned to it. At the end of an accounting period the estimated written-down value of the plant is carried forward to the following period together with work in progress, leaving a charge for depreciation in the contract account. When the contract is completed the residual value of plant is credited to the appropriate contract account and brought back into the head office plant pool.

Because of the long lead time and high value of each contract, it is usually agreed that progress payments be paid by the contractee at progressive stages of completion of work. A surveyor issues a certificate of value of work completed to date, at selling price, from which it is usual to deduct a retention percentage (possibly 10%), to provide for contingent costs that might arise from the need to rectify faulty work. The contractor will then be paid the net amount of the certificate.

Long contract lead times also cause the problem of interim profit measurement, for if a contractor were not to take any profit into account until each contract is finalized, this could lead to some very lean years in which few contracts are completed.

Recommendations on how to deal with this are contained in the accountancy bodies' *Statement of Standard Accounting Practice No. 9*. The overriding principle is that no profit should be attributed to a contract until it can be reasonably forecast. This implies that it would not be prudent to anticipate profit in the early days. Conversely, it is advised that forecast losses should be written off immediately.

Interim profit can be calculated as follows:

Contract price		1,000,000
Less costs to date	300,000	
estimated costs to completion	400,000	
estimated rectification cost	100,000	800,000
Estimated contract profit		£200,000

Assuming that cost of work certified to date is £250,000, profit attributable to the contract to date is as follows:

$$\frac{\text{cost of work certified}}{\text{estimated total cost}} \times \text{estimated profit}$$

$$= \frac{250,000}{800,000} \times 200,000 = £62,500$$

Processed unit cost

Figure 11 illustrates the flow of resources in a processing business and how the cost per unit of output accumulates.

Each process is charged with the cost of resources which can be directly identified with that process. Material will be input into Process 1, together with directly chargeable production labour and expenses. A share of other production- and service department overheads is apportioned to the process, and the total cost (less work-in-progress) transferred to Process 2, where another cycle of processing and cost accumulation is

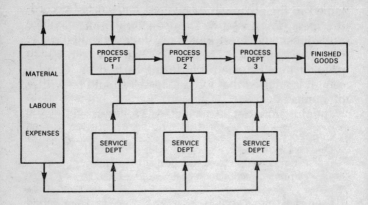

Figure 11. Accumulating process costs

completed. Ultimately, the output from Process 3 is
transferred to finished goods, and the cost per unit will
be a function of total accumulated costs divided by total
finished output.

One of the characteristics of continuous processing
industries is the normal loss suffered in processing.
Unfortunately, when a cost is described as 'normal' it
tends to get little attention, and therefore needs special
control. 1,000 litres of input into a process may normally
yield only 900 litres of output due to evaporation,
chemical change, etc. Anything less than 900 litres is
abnormal and management should be aware of this.
Consequently, abnormal losses (and gains) are high-
lighted in a special overhead account for control
purposes.

Incomplete work may also cause a problem in determining unit cost, as costs incurred to date will relate not
only to finished units, but also to unfinished ones. The
problem can be ignored when stocks are virtually nonexistent or are always at the same level, but not
otherwise. At the end of a financial year, incomplete

work will be physically measured and costed accordingly, but in the interim, control periods, a percentage estimate is sometimes made of the completion stage reached on units in progress. Work in progress is then valued using the concept of 'equivalent units'.

For example, if 1,000 units are put into a process, 10% of input is normally lost, 700 units are transferred to finished goods and 150 units are half-complete at the end of a period, the units will be accounted for as follows:

		Cost £
Finished units	700	1,400 to finished goods
Abnormal loss	50	100 to abnormal loss account
Incomplete units	75	150 carried forward into next period
	825	£1,650

NOTES:

1 abnormal loss is $1,000 - (700 + 100 + 150)$.
2 incomplete units are 50% of 150.
3 assumed that total costs during the period were £1,650, therefore cost per equivalent unit is £1,650 ÷ 825 = £2.

Operating costs

The basic approach to ascertaining cost per unit in service industries is similar to process costing, i.e. total costs are divided by total output, although some industries may adopt more than one output unit. For example, hotels cost their accommodation in terms of occupied bed nights, but their restaurants in meals served. Hospitals use in-patient days to cost their medical wards, but theatre activity is measured per operation.

Cost-centre control is a feature of all service industry

activity, but presentation of unit cost information will differ considerably because of the variety of that activity.

An abbreviated operating statement for an omnibus company is illustrated below, showing the total cost of each category of expense and the cost in pence per mile for each expense.

Stubbs Omnibus Co. Ltd
Operating statement for the month of ....

Expense	£000s	pence per mile
Drivers' and conductors' wages	300	7.50
Uniforms	20	0.50
Tyres	50	1.25
Fuel	60	1.50
Vehicle maintenance	40	1.00
Traffic expenses	40	1.00
Vehicle depreciation	70	1.75
General expenses	20	0.50
	£600	£15.00

8 Estimating Cost Behaviour

The need to know how costs behave

Before we can put a car on the road we have to pay the fixed charges of road-fund tax and insurance. It is only when we drive the car that we incur the costs of petrol, oil, tyres and maintenance – the costs that vary directly with the mileage driven. Similarly, when an organization is committed to a plan of activity, it also commits itself to a planned level of expenditure – sometimes commencing well before the start of operating activity. Rent, rates, insurance, machinery, management salaries and expenses, are prime examples of this type of fixed expenditure.

Other costs will be incurred when operating activity commences, the level of expenditure being generally proportionate to the level of activity. For example, the direct material cost in toy manufacturing will vary directly with the number of toys manufactured.

A word of caution however. A *direct* cost is not always a *variable* cost. By definition, a direct cost is one that can be specifically related to a particular product. Direct material is nearly always variable as one unit of output consumes a standard amount of material. Direct labour may also be used in proportion to volume of output, especially in jobbing type industries; but in processing industries, for example food, where production is continuous and largely governed by the pace of machines, direct labour workers may be classified as fixed. In these circumstances they are largely a team of machine minders and the same number will be required even if production is at half capacity.

Some costs normally thought of as fixed, such as supervisory salaries, may change as output increases. Depreciation is treated as fixed in most circumstances, but in offshore oil operations, oil rigs, with their attendant plant and machinery, are written off in relation to barrels of oil produced.

A knowledge of cost behaviour is fundamental to determining relevant costs for management planning and controlling, especially in the following areas:

- planning the optimum volume of output
- fixing selling prices
- deciding whether to make or buy a component
- formulating budgets for control purposes
- adjusting (flexing) those budgets to facilitate meaningful comparison with actual performance.

Basic cost behaviour

Fixed costs are those that do not change with the level of activity (Figure 12a). They may be long-term committed costs, such as rent, rates, building insurance and depreciation; or be the result of short-term management policy – as in the cases of advertising and research. Expenditure on the latter is discretionary and can be withdrawn at any time without affecting productive capacity. It is the kind of expenditure which is the first to suffer in a cost-cutting campaign.

However, no cost is fixed for ever. A doubling of plant capacity will usually double rent, rates and insurance, and the decision to increase capacity would have to take account of this. Most decisions are concerned with the short-to-medium term however, that is with the current range of activity, within which fixed costs will not change.

A *variable cost* is one that is dependent upon the volume of some activity and which, for most short-term purposes, is assumed to bear a linear relationship with the level of that activity (Figure 12b). The quantity of materials and components used by Rover Cars is directly proportionate to the number of cars manufactured. Electricity consumed by a machine is a function of the number of hours that the machine is running. Sales commission is often a fixed percentage of sales value.

Costs with a mixture of fixed and variable elements are known as *semi-variables*. These include telephones which have a fixed rental plus the variable cost of calls made (Figure 12c).

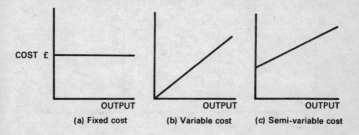

Figure 12. Basic cost behaviour

Non-linear cost behaviour

A very good example of *curvilinear cost* behaviour is that illustrated by the learning curve discussed in Chapter 6 in relation to direct labour. As pointed out, completely new operations will take longer to complete in the early stages, but as workers become more experienced, this time is shortened until labour becomes directly variable to output. A further example of curvilinear behaviour is production scrap cost, which will usually increase at higher levels of production because less time is being spent on quality control (Figure 13a).

Another fairly usual cost is the 'stepped cost', where,

for example, at increasing levels of output, additional supervision will be required (Figure 13b). If these steps are quite short, they can often be interpreted as representing variable behaviour, at least until current full capacity has been reached. The problem is that when orders are low, management will not lightly put the variable process into reverse, unless a permanent reduction in output is planned. Figure 13c illustrates a linear cost that does change its cost per unit, but less frequently than the 'stepped cost'. This is typical of utility charges, where the cost per unit changes after a stated level of consumption is reached.

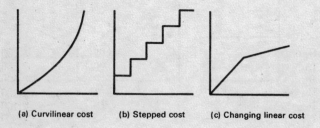

(a) Curvilinear cost   (b) Stepped cost   (c) Changing linear cost

Figure 13. Non-linear cost behaviour

Methods of estimating cost behaviour

Cost-behaviour patterns are generally either flat – over a certain range of activity – or increase proportionate to activity. The flat or fixed costs are fairly easy to spot, being either mandatory payments for all levels of activity, such as rent, or a discretionary payment resulting from management policy, such as advertising. Excepting direct materials, variable costs are not quite so obvious, and semi-variables might be even more obscure.

In this section we look at various ways of analysing cost behaviour.

Analysis of past costs

Examination of past costs is at least objective and provides the starting point for even the most sophisticated statistical techniques of analysis. But past conditions that caused those costs may not continue in the future. Price, technological and organizational changes have to be reflected in the forecasts.

However, a mixture of logic and experience of the operations involved should give a workable approximation of the behaviour pattern of each cost.

The indirect expenses of an engineering company for the past three years have been as follows:

	Cost category	1 £	2 £	3 £
			Years	
Supervision	F	28,000	28,000	28,000
Indirect labour	SV	31,300	34,800	37,500
Indirect materials	V	12,800	16,200	18,600
Scrap	V	1,100	1,400	1,600
Electric power	SV	5,600	6,600	7,100
Depreciation – machines	F	4,000	4,000	4,000
Tools	V	3,400	4,200	5,200
Rent and rates	F	30,000	30,000	30,000
		116,200	125,200	132,000
Direct labour hours worked		17,000	21,000	25,000

F = fixed   V = variable   SV = semi-variable

Note that, in this example, hours worked is the variable which seems to have the greatest influence on each of the costs. This may be a fair approximation in most circumstances, but if any other factor has a stronger influence on a particular cost, it should be taken into account.

Unchanging committed costs, such as rent and rates, are obviously fixed, whilst variable costs are most likely to respond to hours worked and thus to level of output.

Electric power is assumed to be based on a fixed

standard charge plus a variable cost per unit actually used, although other tariffs are available. The same fixed plus variable pattern applies to telephones.

As regards indirect labour, it is assumed that, at the very lowest level of production, a fixed number of indirect workers will be needed, with stepped additional cost thereafter, in tune with production.

Assuming the data above has been adjusted for future price and other changes, we should be able to estimate costs for an output of 23,000 hours, by simple interpolation between the figures for 21,000 and 25,000 hours, as shown below:

	Cost category	£
Supervision	F	28,000
Indirect labour	SV	36,150
Indirect materials	V	17,400
Scrap	V	1,500
Electric power	SV	6,850
Depreciation – machines	F	4,000
Tools	V	4,700
Rent and rates	F	30,000
		£128,600

Engineered costs

The most scientific way of establishing a cost standard is by applying work-study techniques to the activity giving rise to the cost. The techniques are largely applied to direct labour because the relationship between its activity and production is easily recognized and can therefore be measured. Time and motion studies are made of each task element in a job, the total of all the element times being the standard time allowed for completion of that job. The same information can also be used as the basis for a production incentive scheme, and in standard costing, which is a system for controlling costs (to be dealt with later).

Similarly, an analysis of product specifications and actual working experience can establish a standard direct material cost for each unit of output.

The application of these methods is being increasingly extended to office tasks in today's 'electronic office', where engineered times can be set for repetitive tasks produced by word processor. For example, in an insurance office a standard might be set for the production of so many policies in one hour on the word processor.

High-low method

This method examines costs at high and low levels of activity, making the assumption that the increase in cost between the two levels is directly due to the increase in activity and therefore represents the variable cost. Dividing that increase in cost by the increase in volume of activity between the high and low levels, should give the variable cost per unit of activity.

Taking electric power in the cost schedule in the previous section we have:

	Costs £	Hours
Year 3	7,100	25,000
Year 1	5,600	17,000
	1,500	8,000

Dividing the increase in costs by the increase in hours between the two years, we get: £1,500 ÷ 8,000 = £0.1875 which represents the variable cost per hour.

We then calculate the variable cost of one of the activity levels, say Year 3, and by deducting the resultant figure from the total cost in that year we are left with the fixed cost. This can be checked by carrying out the same calculation on the costs of Year 1.

Total cost	£7,100
less variable cost 25,000 × 0.1875	4,688
Fixed cost	£2,412

The cost function for electric power is therefore £2,412 + £0.1875 per hour. For 23,000 hours this would be £6,724, which compares with our interpolated estimate of £6,850.

Scattergraph analysis

The major drawback to the high-low approach is that it ascribes a straight-line function between the highest and lowest points, which may not necessarily be a true representation of the cost behaviour between those two points, and, more probably, will not represent the cost at extremely high and low levels of output.

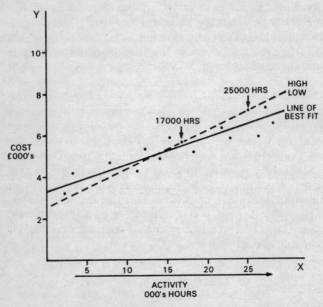

Figure 14. Scattergraph cost chart

Scattergraph analysis can help here. The cost/activity co-ordinates drawn from past records are plotted on to a graph and a visual best-fitting line is drawn through these points (Figure 14), so that the total distances between all the points above the line equal those below it.

Fixed cost is where the sloping line crosses the vertical (Y) axis, and the variable cost per hour is represented by the gradient of the line drawn through the points. Thus $Y = a + bX$.

The high-low line has been added to the graph to show how it misleads when compared with the line of best fit. The latter is a more accurate picture of past cost behaviour, showing fixed cost at a higher figure and variable cost per hour, lower.

Statistical regression analysis

Linear regression is a mathematical technique from which the cost function $Y = a + bX$ can be derived. It is commonly known as the *method of least squares* because it equates the sum of the squared distances above the line to those below the line. It adds more accuracy to the fitting of the cost line than can be achieved by a visual fit, and can be calculated easily by desk calculator. Micro-computer packages are also available to speed the task, and provide a facility to test sensitivity to change.

Multiple regression analysis recognizes that cost may be a function of more than one variable. For example, the volume of sales is influenced by price, advertising, packaging, income levels, the state of the economy, substitutes, and so on. A standard computer package is available to deal with this.

9 Cost, Volume and Profit Analysis

What is contribution?

Business strategic planning normally involves investment decisions aimed at providing the most economic
mix of resources to achieve long-term organizational
goals. Planning is vital because the installation of additional plant, machinery and buildings is often subject to
long delivery and constructional delays.

Whilst additional capacity is awaited, however, technology, competition and general economic conditions
may change, and have to be reflected in short-term
profit planning. This will necessitate the consideration
of alternative sales and production scenarios, leading to
short-term decisions on the level of advertising and
other expenditure, selling prices, and production
volumes, summarized in forecast profit and loss
accounts.

The cost, volume and profit (CVP) analysis required in
the preparation of these profit and loss accounts
includes the same cost inputs used to ascertain total cost
per unit (see Chapter 7), but separates fixed and variable
costs as follows:

Marginal profit and loss account

		Total £	per unit £
Sales (10,000 units)		200,000	20
less variable costs:			
manufacturing	90,000		
selling	20,000		
administration	10,000	120,000	12
Contribution		80,000	8
less fixed costs:			
manufacturing	30,000		
selling	5,000		
administration	5,000	40,000	
Net profit		£ 40,000	

In the conventional profit and loss account (see page 2) manufacturing product costs are consolidated into one figure and deducted from sales to give gross profit. Selling and administration period costs are then deducted to give net profit. The net profit will be the same in both the conventional and marginal statements if there is no change in stock levels, but if stocks do change, profits will differ by the amount of fixed manufacturing cost transferred into or out of stock.

For CVP analysis purposes the *marginal* or 'contribution' format is more helpful because it shows more clearly the contribution made towards (a) fixed costs – those that do not change with volume of output – and (b) profit. Analysed by products or departments, this information becomes a powerful profit planning tool.

The mathematics of CVP analysis

The figures in the marginal statement in the previous section can be summarized in the following form:

(selling price × sales volume) − (variable cost × sales volume) −fixed costs = net profit

or Sx − Vx − FC = NP

and substituting the figures in that statement we have:

$(20 \times 10,000) - (12 \times 10,000) - 40,000 = £40,000$

This simple profit equation can be applied to any problem involving any of the variables, or prospective changes in them. Examples of its application follow, using the data already given.

1 *What minimum volume of sales is required to cover fixed costs?*

Since no profit is expected at this level it can be omitted and the equation rewritten:

$(S − V)x = FC$

or $(20 − 12)x = 40,000$

∴ $8x = 40,000$

and   x = 5,000 units (or 5,000 × £20 sales value = £100,000)

x is, of course, the breakeven volume, and it can be deduced from the above workings that this is the number of product contributions required to recover fixed costs, i.e. £40,000 ÷ 8 = £5,000.

Another way of calculating breakeven volume expressed in sales value, is to ascertain the *contribution to sales ratio* (CS Ratio) and divide it into fixed costs. In the above example the CS ratio is 8/20 × 100 = 40%, and breakeven sales volume 40,000 ÷ 0.40 = £100,000, which confirms the figure calculated earlier.

2 *How many units have to be sold to realize a profit of £60,000?*

Using the original net profit equation we have:

$$Sx - Vx - FC = £60,000$$
$$\text{and } 20x - 12x - 40,000 = £60,000$$
$$8x = £100,000$$
$$x = £12,500$$

Proof: 12,500 × 8 (contribution) less £40,000 (fixed costs)
= £60,000 (profit)

3 *Would it be worth spending an additional £20,000 on advertising if, as a result, the number of units sold increased by 2,000?*

Here we treat the advertising as an additional fixed cost:

$$(20 \times 12,000) - (12 \times 12,000) - 40,000 - 20,000 = NP$$
$$240,000 - 144,000 - 40,000 - 20,000 = NP$$
$$36,000 = NP$$

The result would be to reduce profit by £4,000, therefore the advertising would not be implemented.

Another way to reach the same result:

Additional cost − additional contribution
= £20,000   − (2,000 × 8)
= £4,000 loss

4 *Would it be worth reducing selling price by £1 if this resulted in an increase in sales of 3,000 units?*

In this problem we reduce selling price (S) by £1 and increase volume by 3,000

$$(19 \times 13,000) - (12 \times 13,000) - 40,000 = NP$$
$$247,000 - 156,000 - 40,000 = NP$$
$$£51,000 = NP$$

showing an increase in profit of £11,000 , which justifies the proposed action.

5 *If variable cost is forecast to increase by £1 per unit,
fixed cost by £11,000 and selling price cannot be
increased, how many units will have to be sold to realize
the same profit as last year?*

Increase variable cost per unit and fixed cost accordingly

$$(20x - 13x) - 51,000 = 40,000$$
$$7x = 91,000$$
$$x = 13,000$$

therefore units sold will have to increase by 3,000 to
absorb the cost increases.

CVP analysis is graphical form

Management can be given an instant picture of the
relationship between costs and profit at different
volumes of sales, by construction of a simple chart
(Figure 15).

Total costs and sales revenue are shown on the vertical axis, and sales volume in units on the horizontal.
Commencing with zero output variable cost at £12 per
unit increases in direct proportion to sales. Fixed costs
of £40,000 form a layer above and parallel with variable
cost, to give a total cost line at any level of sales.

If the sales function is then added, commencing at
zero and increasing by £20 for each additional unit sold,
the resultant sales revenue line is seen to cross the total
cost line. At this point total sales equals total costs, there
is neither profit nor loss – this is the *'breakeven' point*.
Sales volumes below it show a loss because costs are not
all recovered, and volumes above it a profit, because
costs are more than recovered. The total profit or loss
can be measured vertically between the sales and total
cost lines at any volume of sales.

For example, at 10,000 units, the profit of £40,000
shown in the profit and loss account at the beginning of

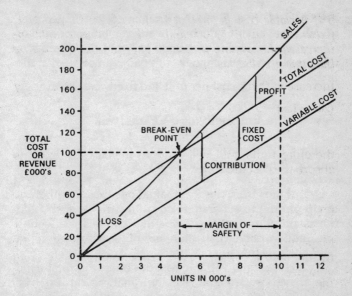

Figure 15. Contribution and breakeven chart

this chapter, can be confirmed by the chart. It is the distance between total costs of £160,000 and the sales line at £200,000. Likewise, the breakeven point is confirmed at 5,000 units.

The picture of contribution, i.e. the difference between the sales and variable cost lines, is clearly shown – nibbling away at fixed costs until they are completely recovered at the breakeven point.

One further useful piece of information is the measurement of the *'margin of safety'*. This is the difference between the current maximum level of sales and the breakeven point. It shows by how much sales can fall before a loss is suffered, and is usually expressed as a percentage, i.e. sales value above the breakeven point divided by total sales × 100; in this example 50%.

The microcomputer is particularly suitable for

presenting CVP analysis to management. Packaged programs are available which allow manipulation of each or all of the variables in response to 'what if?' questions. Results of proposed changes in policy can be seen at the press of a button.

Beware the simplicity of CVP analysis

Whilst CVP analysis can aid management in decision-making, it has to be applied with care and knowledge of its limitations.

Quite apart from the approximations that are inherent in attempting to separate fixed from variable costs, and the assumption that volume is the only factor affecting sales and variable cost, there are other assumptions in CVP analysis that limit its usefulness.

If no changes in variable cost per unit or in total fixed cost are envisaged, the resultant analysis can only be valid within the volume range covered by these unchanging cost conditions. In addition, changes in technology, efficiency and competition are ignored.

In the form presented, therefore, it is applicable only to making short-term decisions affecting one product, or several products where the same proportionate sales mix is expected over the planned total output range.

We do not have to be tied to straight lines however. If variable cost per unit is lower at lower levels of production and increases at higher levels, this can be depicted, as can any change in fixed costs, perhaps of a 'stepped' nature. Allowance can also be made for a lowering of selling price to increase sales.

Figure 16 incorporates these more realistic curvilinear cost and revenue factors, as well as a 'stepped' increase in fixed costs. In particular, the output level at which profit is optimized can be observed.

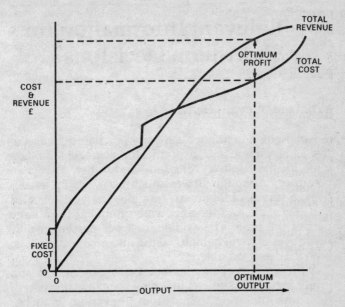

Figure 16. CVP chart with curvilinear functions

Computer simulation

Although Figure 16 is more realistic than the previous breakeven chart, the more sophisticated analysis required calls for a higher level of computation. Fortunately the flexibility and speed of the micro-computer can be called to the rescue again. Financial modelling programmes are available to simulate the process of combining variables to forecast possible outcomes of different actions.

10 Relevant Information for Short-term Decisions

What are relevant costs?

A well-known insurance company purchased an executive jet aeroplane to transport its top managers to meetings in the United Kingdom and other European countries. Although it was much used by top executives, a survey of flights covering the first year revealed that the plane and its crew were grounded for a large part of the time. The average cost per passenger-mile flown was extremely high, taking into account all costs, both fixed and variable.

A further survey of general travelling by middle and junior managers showed that they spent a major part of their time motoring to and from the various branches and customers of the company, frequently having to stay at expensive hotels overnight.

A few simple calculations convinced the company's transport officer that it would be more economic to increase the mileage travelled by the company jet, to transport some of its junior and middle managers on business. The relevant costs in this decision were those specifically incurred because of the additional miles flown, including fuel, maintenance and airport landing fees. Crew costs were already committed, depreciation was a sunk cost, and these were therefore not relevant. In addition, the alternative costs of motoring and hotels were reckoned as savings.

The transport cost review did not end there, however. It was estimated that employees selling company insurance products and using the jet service would be able to double their turnover, because a large part of their previous travelling time could be used fruitfully to sell insurance.

Paradoxically, the net result of their expensive jet flying more miles, would be increased profit for the company – a good illustration of applying only the relevant costs and revenues to short-term decisions, the guiding principles of which can be summarized as follows:

- costs incurred in the past are not relevant, i.e. they are sunk costs, such as an aeroplane already paid for
- costs that will be incurred whether the decision is taken or not, i.e. committed costs such as salaries of permanent aircrew are not relevant
- decisions are between alternatives, if only to do or not to do a particular thing; therefore only the differences in costs and benefits are relevant. Costs common to both, such as the rent of a hangar to house an aircraft, are thus irrelevant
- include the cost of lost revenue, i.e. opportunity cost – continued under-utilization of the jet, for example, would lose the company valuable sales.

'Short term' is relative of course. CVP analysis regards variable cost per unit and fixed cost as unchanging over the planned range of output. At high output levels, increased fixed costs could be incurred and, additionally, fixed assets will inevitably need to be replaced. In the context of our jet aeroplane example, when the time comes to consider replacement of the aircraft, its replacement cost will certainly be relevant to the investment decision.

Construction or replacement of assets may involve long delays, therefore the best possible use must be made of existing resources without compromising long-term goals.

Decisions that might be taken in the short term include:

- shall we make or buy a product?
- shall we keep open or close down a department or other activity?
- should we reject orders?
- given limited resources, what sales mix will optimize profit?

Make or buy?

Due to environmental laws, Hemming Agriculture plc are forced to incorporate an anti-pollution device in the manufacture of a special one-off batch of 4,000 petrol-engine powered 'Mammoth' motor mowers destined for open parkland customers in the United States. A supplier offers Hemming this unit at a price of £150 each, which compares with internal costs per unit as follows:

	£
Direct materials and components	60
Direct labour	40
Indirect labour – variable	10
Other variable manufacturing overhead	40
Fixed manufacturing overhead	30
Variable selling costs	10
Fixed selling costs	15
	£205

NOTES:

1 Variable overhead is directly related to labour hours.
2 The company is working at below full capacity at the moment, due to lack of orders, but management have agreed that skilled direct labour will be retained, indirect labour can be signed on and off as required.

3 Fixed costs are apportionments of total company overheads.

If a business has spare capacity, the make or buy decision rests essentially upon a comparison of the incremental costs of making, with the price offered by the outside supplier.

In Hemming's case the following internal costs are relevant:

		£
1	Direct materials/components	60
2	Direct labour	—
3	Indirect labour – variable	10
4	Other variable manufacturing overheads	40
5	Variable selling overhead	10
6	Fixed costs	—
		£120

Reasons for including/excluding items are that:

1 is an additional cost caused by making
2 is a committed expenditure – without this order
3 is specially engaged for this contract
4 involves more out-of-pocket cost
5 also involves more out-of-pocket cost
6 would be incurred whether or not this work proceeds.

If, however, Hemming is working at full capacity, but decides to go ahead with this additional work by displacing other work, the contribution that would be made by this other work should be treated as an opportunity cost of the new contract and added to the relevant costs listed above.

Most decisions of the 'make or buy' variety are as much influenced by qualitative factors as quantitative ones, and any of the following may tip the scale in favour of making:

- a desire to retain a skilled labour force
- the need to control quality
- the need to ensure continuity of supply
- the necessity to retain secrecy of processing techniques
- the possibility that the supplier may increase his price at a later date
- a need to control production.

Keep open or close down?

A photographic and electrical goods store operates four departments. A summary profit and loss account for last year is given below:

			£000s		
	A	B	C	D	Total
Sales	200	400	160	500	1,260
Cost of goods sold	120	200	80	280	680
Fixed selling costs	48	20	30	30	128
Fixed admin. costs	45	80	40	90	255
Net profit (loss)	(13)	100	10	100	197

Management is considering whether to close down the 'loss-making' Department A, and possibly C, whose return on capital invested in stocks and display equipment is disappointing.

Investigation reveals that the fixed costs specifically incurred by the departments are £30, £10, £10 and £20 respectively. Each of these costs could be avoided if the relative department were to cease operations. All the other fixed selling and administration costs would continue.

A more revealing contribution statement was produced by the management accountant as shown below:

	A	B	C	D	Total
			£000s		
Sales	200	400	160	500	1,260
Cost of goods sold	120	200	80	280	680
Fixed costs – directly attributable	30	10	10	20	70
Contribution	50	190	70	200	510

Other fixed costs:	
selling	58
admin.	255
Net profit	£197

OBSERVATIONS:

1 All departments are making contributions towards fixed costs and profit.
2 If A is closed down the business will lose its contribution of £50,000.
3 Sales in other departments might be directly affected should A close down.
4 Department C also makes a substantial contribution and probably encourages customers to purchase related equipment.
5 Directly attributable fixed costs are relevant to the calculation of contribution; other fixed costs are not.
6 If floor space used by departments A and C can be used to generate a higher contribution if used to sell some other product or to expand existing activities, closing them down would be the correct decision. Even then, the interdependence of the sales of other departments cannot be ignored in making the decision.

Should we ever reject orders?

The answer to this question depends upon the comparative contributions from the alternative use of resources.

Given full-capacity working, and that a potential customer's order cannot be delayed or subcontracted, the decision will rest upon whether a contribution is realized after taking account, not only of sales revenue and incremental costs of the new order, but also the opportunity cost (i.e. contribution foregone) associated with the alternative use of the production resources.

For example, if a bus company received separate inquiries for the hire of their last available forty-seater coach for use on the same day, the one yielding the highest potential contribution would be accepted. The comparative figures might be as follows:

		£
Hire of coach to local college		250
less variable cost	130	
opportunity cost of alternative use	90	220
Excess contribution		£30

If a firm has spare capacity, additional work should be undertaken as long as the price received is at least equal to the additional cost incurred in doing the work.

For example, Woodside Engineering produce a valve which currently sells for £40, and the costs of which are:

	£
Direct materials	8
Direct labour	6
Variable manufacturing overhead	2
Variable selling overhead	5
Total fixed overhead	5
	£26

Variable selling overhead includes 10% commission on sales value.

The company is currently operating at 80% capacity, but it has decided to retain all its skilled direct workers for the next twelve months.

An inquiry is received from Jones' Motors for the supply of 2,000 valves of similar specification to the standard valve, but which will require the fitting of a small additional component. Luckily, Woodside have 2,000 of these components in stock which cost them £1 each a year ago, but would cost £2 each to replace now. If Jones' Motors did not take the valves, Woodside would scrap the components because they have no other use.

Jones' offers to pay £20 each for the valves. Should the order be accepted?

The incremental costs of the proposed order are as follows:

		£
		£
Direct materials		8
Variable overhead:		
manufacturing	2	
selling	3	5
		£13

NOTES:

1 The cost of the additional component is nil because if not used it would be scrapped.
2 Direct labour will be paid whether this order goes ahead or not.
3 Variable selling overhead includes 10% of £20 commission, plus £1 remaining of the original figure after excluding sales commission of £4.
4 All fixed costs are already committed and are not relevant.

The order should be accepted because it contributes 2,000 × (£20 − 13) = £14,000 to profit, but, only if the following conditions also apply:

- the Jones' order might lead to more profitable follow-on orders, even though an alternative use of existing spare capacity might be more profitable in the short term
- the sale of the special value to Jones' will not have a depressive effect on prices in the main valve market
- no other work is available which will yield a higher contribution.

Single limiting factor and product mix

As a general rule, long-term profitability ought not to be sacrificed to short-term gain. That said, a business will normally concentrate its limited resources on the mix of products or services that maximizes contribution.

Given the following data regarding the three products of a company, on which product should it concentrate most of its resources?

	Product A	B	C
	£	£	£
Sales price	50	72	30
Variable cost	30	40	15
Contribution	20	32	15
Sales demand	15,000	10,000	12,000

If maximizing contribution is the aim of the company and product sales are not interdependent, it appears that the company should produce according to contribution ranking, i.e. B first (until sales demand for the product is satisfied), then A, then C. If all products use the same quantity of scarce resource per unit in their manufacture, this decision would be correct, but if this is not the case, the products should be ranked in order of contribution per limiting factor.

Presuming labour hours to be the constraint, the contributions per labour hour worked are:

	A	B	C
	£	£	£
Contribution per unit	20	32	15
Labour hours per unit	4	8	2
Contribution per limiting factor	5	4	7.5

which reverses the ranking of the previous decision.

Say labour hours available are limited to 100,000, production and contribution would be:

Product	Production	Labour hours required	Contribution £000s
C	12,000	24,000	180
A	15,000	60,000	300
B	2,000	16,000	64
		100,000	£544

Note that the production of B is limited to 2,000 units.

Such a decision is rarely based solely on quantitative factors, however. Other influences that are difficult to quantify and are therefore qualitative by nature, will also have to be weighed in the decision. These influences will include:

- demand for products being interdependent, which will mean that reducing sales on one may reduce turnover on another
- one or more products being closed down, which may encourage competitors to take up lost orders or lose valuable customer goodwill

- shortage of capacity being overcome by working overtime, shift work or subcontracting.

More than one limiting factor and product mix

Businesses should plan to install resources to meet long-term demand, then, if everything goes according to plan, there ought not to be any constraints on production. Actual and planned practice have a disconcerting habit of deviating however, and businesses often find themselves with not just one limiting factor, but two or more.

In these circumstances a mathematical technique known as *linear programming* can be used to determine optimum output and, if there are more than two constraints, a computer program is necessary, but readily available, to solve the problem.

Where there are only two limiting factors the optimum output can be solved by the graphical method – see Figure 17 below.

Assume that a firm makes two products, D and E, with contributions of £10 and £8 respectively. Production hours required for each product, and total labour and machine hours available to the firm are as follows:

	——per unit——	
Product	Labour hours	Machine hours
D	4	1.5
E	2	3
Hours available	4,000	3,000

The first step is to formulate the problem and this is shown as follows:

1 Maximize $10D + 8E$
2 Subject to: $4D + 2E \leqslant 4,000$
3            $1.5D + 3E \leqslant 3,000$

NOTES:

1 is the *objective function*, which is describing the optimum contribution.
2 describes the labour hours constraint.
3 describes the machine hours constraint.

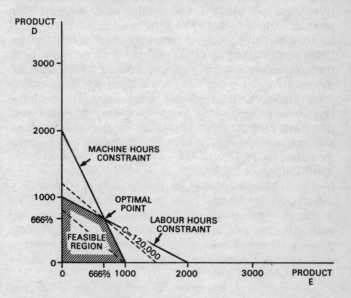

Figure 17. Linear programming maximum contribution graph

The two products are then represented on the graph in Figure 17, D on the vertical and E on the horizontal axis.

Taking the labour-hour limitation first, it can be seen that we can produce a maximum of $4,000 \div 4 = 1,000$ Ds; or a maximum of $4,000 \div 2 = 2,000$ Es; or a combination of both the products in between these two extremes.

This result can be graphed as shown above, a straight line joining the two possible maximum outputs, with combinations of D and E in between the two points.

Similarly, for machine hours, the maximum outputs of 2,000 Ds and 1,000 Es are joined, to show all possible production mixes of the two products.

The area inside the boundaries, formed by the two constraint lines and the horizontal and vertical axes, is the 'feasible region' because it contains all possible production combinations, with the optimum solution lying at one of the corners of this area.

To find which corner, we first draw a broken line between two points on D and E which will yield the same contribution. For example, we could start with 800 Ds and 1,000 Es, each of which gives £8,000 contribution. Then, moving the line to the right parallel with the first line, progressively increases the contribution until the most extreme point of the feasible region is reached. This is noted in Figure 17 as the 'optimum point', comprising 666 of D and 666 of E, giving the maximum contribution of £12,000.

The very description of this analytical approach – linear programming – hints at its limitations. Like CVP analysis it presumes an unchanging selling price and variable cost per unit, and static resources and technology. It therefore applies to only the short term, as most variables and constraints can be modified in the medium to long term.

Despite this, it is a powerful tool and can be adapted to optimize situations where many more constraints exist, by using a microcomputer and an appropriate programme.

11   Costs and Selling prices

INTRODUCTION

The assumption that the long-term objective of a business is to earn an adequate return on the capital it employs, implies that all costs must be covered by sales prices in the long term. Profit, then, is the difference between total sales and total costs.

We saw at the end of the last chapter how businesses plan to produce the mix and volumes of products that will maximize profit. This implies a knowledge, not only of costs, but also of selling prices, and whilst costs can be reasonably forecast if product specifications and production technology are known, selling prices can be more of an unknown quantity.

Selling price influences customer demand, but because of the basic fixed and variable behaviour of costs, and economies of scale, unit cost will vary at different levels of demand. We have, then, the proverbial 'chicken and egg' problem. How can an optimum selling price be determined when the cost per unit is indirectly influenced by selling price?

In conditions of *perfect competition*, buyers and sellers of a commodity or service are instantly aware of changes in price, supply or demand, and react promptly to such changes. An individual supplier produces only a small part of the total supply and cannot influence price by increasing or decreasing output. He has to take the price given by the market and is therefore left only with the problem of estimating the level of output to maximize his profit. Perfect market conditions are not general, however, but mainly relate to commodities such as wheat, currencies and marketable (quoted) securities.

When a market is dominated by a few large firms, all suppliers in the market will be obliged to accept the price established by the market leaders. Under these conditions of *oligopoly*, e.g. in the petrol distribution industry, suppliers will probably suffer losses in their share of the market if they increase prices, and will not gain by price cutting as competitors will quickly follow suit. Profit margins can then only be widened by intensive sales promotion, cost efficiency or opening up new channels of distribution, e.g. mail order instead of direct selling.

Although the market conditions described above may exist, the majority of businesses do have some room for manoeuvre in setting their selling prices, but they have the same aims as the firms who are obliged to take market prices. That is, they:

- fix the level of output of each product at the point where the difference between its total revenue and total cost is greatest (see Figure 16, Chapter 9), subject, however, to constraints caused by limiting factors
- plan for a profit level which is at least equal to the minimum required rate of return on capital employed.

Selling prices in the short term

In the long run, all costs are relevant and long-term pricing policy should take them into account. Conditions may arise in the short term, however, that require a less than full cost view to be taken.

In Chapter 10 we considered whether a firm should accept an order if a potential customer insists on offering a price lower than the normal selling price. In times of recession and under-capacity working, the answer is yes – as long as the stated price is at least equal to the incremental costs of production.

If goods are already manufactured but in excess of customers' requirements, the minimum price to charge is zero; any price above that will provide a welcome additional contribution.

New but potentially valuable customers may also be offered a special price for a pilot order, on condition that the concession will not compromise the future pricing policy of the product concerned or any other product in the catalogue. In these circumstances, the minimum price should not be less than the incremental production costs, plus any opportunity cost (i.e. contribution lost) of using the production facilities for some other purpose.

Marketing strategy and pricing policy

Though pricing policy has a significant influence on demand, it has to be seen as part of a total marketing strategy. No matter what price tag is put on an article, if the customer is not attracted by it, the till will not ring up a sale. Product design, quality and packaging must appeal to potential customers, and the two can only be matched by appropriate market research into customer requirements. Pricing may, then, be more influenced by the segment of the market to be satisfied, than by production costs.

Sales promotion strategy in the form of advertising and special offers, may also influence customer demand more effectively than pricing policy.

Setting 'normal' selling prices

The pricing manager may approach his task of setting product selling prices in two ways:

1 he may adopt the economic approach and attempt to estimate demand at different prices, together with an analysis of costs and profit at each level of demand (CVP analysis, Chapter 9).
2 he may estimate the cost of a product at the expected sales volume and add an appropriate profit mark-up.

In the first approach he will be attempting to ascertain the price level that will optimize profit (Figure 16, Chapter 9); whilst the second pricing method assumes a level of demand and then develops a cost-plus price based on that assumption.

Demand analysis

Here we assume imperfect market conditions, i.e. that sales volume will increase as price is reduced. The rate of increase will be partly a function of the *elasticity of demand* for the product. Elasticity is an economic concept referring to the effect on demand of changes in price. As a generalization, the demand for necessities such as bread, is inelastic; whereas demand for luxuries such as jewellery will be more sensitive to price changes and are therefore said to be elastic. The measure of elasticity is largely dependent upon the existence or absence of substitutes for the product or service, the number of consumers and their general level of income.

To the analysis of volume at different prices is then added the relevant fixed and variable costs at each level of output, and the contribution at each sales volume, as shown in the table below:

All figures in 000s (except selling price)

Selling price	Volume units	Total sales (1)	Variable costs (2)	Specific fixed costs (3)	Contribution (1 – (2+3))
£		£	£	£	£
4	18	72	70	7	(5)
5	18	90	70	7	13
6	18	108	70	7	31
7	15	105	57	7	41
8	10	80	38	5	37
9	7	63	28	5	30
10	4	40	16	5	19
11	1	11	4	5	2

Maximum contribution is realized at 15,000 units at a selling price of £7 per unit, therefore this is the optimum price. But note that all prices above £5 make a contribution towards unavoidable fixed costs. At £4, a loss would be suffered, and at £11 the contribution is probably inadequate. Note also that demand for the product is inelastic between £4 and £6.

Demand analysis is theoretically sound, but pins a lot of faith in the forecaster's ability to predict the demand curve for each product. There is also the problem of assigning scarce resources to maximize total contribution (see linear programming, Chapter 10).

Cost plus mark-up

Surveys in the United Kingdom and the United States have found that the majority of business adopt a 'cost-plus' basis for setting selling prices. They would agree that demand and contribution analysis provides useful and relevant information for the pricing decision, but that it is objected to because (a) it could result in under or over pricing because of the difficulty of forecasting demand at different prices, (b) it ignores the unavoidable fixed costs and (c) it may not provide an adequate return on capital employed because it ignores capital investment in each product.

A full-cost selling price make-up is illustrated below:

Selling price make-up Product D
(Assuming Sales volume of 10,000 units)

	£	per unit
Direct materials	15,000	1.50
Direct labour	40,000	4.00
Variable manufacturing overhead	6,273	.63
Total variable manufacturing cost	61,273	6.13
Manufacturing fixed overhead	16,000	1.60
Manufacturing cost	77,273	7.73
Administration and selling overhead	7,727	.77
Total cost	85,000	8.50
Profit mark-up	20,000	2.00
Proposed selling price	£105,000	10.50

NOTES:

1 Manufacturing fixed overhead has been added at 40% of labour cost.
2 Administration and selling overhead has been added at 10% of manufacturing cost.
3 Profit is added at 20% of total capital invested in the product.

The percentage addition for manufacturing fixed overhead can be calculated by relating the estimated total of those costs to the estimated total direct labour cost for the coming year. The administration oncost is similarly calculated – as a percentage of budgeted manufacturing cost for the coming year. Variable selling overheads, such as sales commission, would normally be shown separately in the price make-up.

The profit mark-up should ideally be based upon the capital invested in the particular product, applying the rate of return appropriate to the risk of the product. In the illustration above, a 20% return on capital of £100,000 is required.

The main objection levelled at cost-plus pricing is that it ignores demand at different prices. Used with blinkers on it probably does, but no professional pricing manager sets a selling price without considering its effect on customers and competitors.

Another objection is the arbitrary apportionment of fixed costs to products which hides its true contribution. However, if we look upon budgeted fixed costs as a burden that has to be carried by all production in the coming year, apportionment on an appropriate labour-hour or machine-hour basis can be interpreted as an opportunity cost – the amount that has to be charged if the firm is to achieve its budget.

Knowledge of product variable cost can be very useful to the pricing manager. In the above example, product variable cost is £6.13, and the difference between this and the potential selling price is its contribution towards fixed costs and profit. Given that the total of fixed costs and required profit is £43,727, it is an easy matter to calculate the sales volume that would recover this amount at varying selling prices.

For example, if price was reduced to £9, product contribution would be £9 − 6.13= £2.87, and if we divide this figure into £43,727 the resulting figure of 15,236, is the number of units which have to be sold to realize the required total contribution. The manager has to consider whether that number can be sold at £9, and he would also test the sensitivity of other price changes.

This does bring full-cost pricing nearer to demand analysis, but the supporters of full-cost pricing could argue that taking required profit and fixed costs into the computation is more objective in that it counters the possibility of under pricing.

Price differentiation

All around us there are many examples of the same products and services carrying different selling prices. In the local produce market, fruit and vegetables can be bought at different prices according to the location of the stall; cinema seats are sold at specially low prices to attract children, pensioners and the unemployed; and British Rail has a confusion of attractive off-peak travel fares.

Price differentiation can be practised as long as distinct segments of the market for the same product can be distinguished. Given the fixity of some costs, any additional contribution made by differentiating prices will increase profit.

Price differentiating can be applied in various ways:

1 *Special customers* – special prices may be negotiated with large customers, such as supermarkets and department stores, on an 'own-brand label' basis, or with any customer buying in bulk. Special theatre prices can be arranged for parties of students, pensioners or school children.

2 *Location* – as discussed above, different prices may be quoted in different geographical areas. Examples are petrol prices, which vary to some degree between country and town, prime selling sites and poor sites; and the same model of car which can be bought at different prices at home and overseas.

3 *Time* – off-peak prices are offered for travel, accommodation, holidays and entertainment; lower prices are sometimes charged early in the life cycle of a product to penetrate the market, are then increased when demand is established, then reduced again at the tail end of the cycle to stimulate demand; higher prices are sometimes charged at the launch of a product, during the 'novelty' period, in anticipation of an early

drop in demand, when price will have to be reduced accordingly.

4 *Product differentiation* – qualitative differences in the same product may warrant different prices.

5 *Special offers* – these are designed to boost sales to the same customers, or to attract new customers, e.g. in supermarkets and door-to-door selling. Stores often sell goods at variable cost or below, as 'loss leaders', to entice customers into the store.

12 Budgeting Procedure and Standards

INTRODUCTION

Management information is required for planning and controlling, and so far our emphasis has been on identifying the costs and revenues relevant to long- and short-term decision making. Chapter 6 did deviate from this theme to the extent that it described the techniques and systems for allocating and controlling inputs into business operations – with particular reference to manufacturing – whilst Chapter 7 examined the approaches to ascertaining the total cost of producing a unit of output.

We now turn our attention to short-range operational control of an organization through the use of budgets and standards.

The nature and usefulness of budgets

A budget can be defined as 'a quantitative expression of the operational plans of an organization for a future accounting period'.

The budget is both a *plan of action* and a *control medium*. As a plan, it stipulates targets for sales, output, stocks, cash, etc., which the responsible manager translates into action. As a control medium, it is used to compare with actual performance, for the purpose of assessing the need to take corrective action.

Budgets usually cover a period of one year, as in the case of the national budget presented by the Chancellor of the Exchequer, but they might be prepared to coincide with seasonal needs. For example, fashion and footwear firms budget for six-monthly periods coinciding with seasonal fashion changes. In addition, for finer monitoring of performance, the total budget is normally broken down into monthly, four-weekly or even weekly control periods.

As plans are implemented and operations proceed, the control phase comes into its own. Periodic reports to responsible managers provide them with the guidance needed to attain the original plan. If the plan is not subject to too much change, the control information will indicate that a 'touch of the accelerator' here, and a 'wee bit of braking' there, will keep the plan steadily on course.

When volatile changes in customer demand, resource cost or availability are the normal conditions faced by an organization, however, planning and controlling, certainly in the short term, come face to face. Their juxtaposition is always more evident in times of rapid change and uncertainty.

To deal with swiftly changing conditions, a system of *'rolling budgets'* is used by some firms. Figure 18 illustrates its operation. The long-range plan will be revised on a 'rolling' basis each year. That is, the plans for years 2 to 4 will be reviewed at the end of year 1 and a further year added. The annual short-term budget is determined in the usual way, but at each review date, say quarterly, a revised 'forecast' is produced for the remainder of the budget period, plus a further quarter. Thus the plans are 'rolled' forward.

LONG-TERM 4-YEAR PLAN	YEAR 1						YEAR 2			YEAR 3	YEAR 4
SHORT-TERM 1-YEAR BUDGET	QTR 1	QTR 2	QTR 3	QTR 4							
FORECAST AT END OF PERIOD 1	ACTUAL	F O R E C A S T									
FORECAST AT END OF PERIOD 2	ACTUAL	ACTUAL	F O R E C A S T								

Figure 18. The 'rolling' budget

Control reports at each review date will show comparisons of actual, budget and forecast results, with a lot more credence placed on the comparison of actual with 'forecast', than of actual with budget results. The emphasis is upon controlling the future rather than the past. Rolling budgets can be justified on the grounds that:

- conditions can change drastically within a year, especially in times of high inflation, therefore pricing and other policies need to be reviewed frequently
- an annual review is too limiting in rapidly changing conditions
- budgets and standards tend to be set on the high side when they refer to a long, uncertain period ahead.

Obviously, the periodic reviews cause additional analytical and clerical work, therefore one has to be fairly certain that the benefits to be derived from the system are worth its cost. Fortunately, the development of low-cost microcomputers has brought the possibility of this more dynamic mode of control within the range of relatively small organizations.

The usefulness of budgets can be summarized as follows. They:

- compel management to think ahead about sales and production, and the resources required
- communicate the plans of the organization
- assign responsibility to functional managers for the implementation and realization of plans
- allow managers to participate fully in the preparation of plans and therefore motivate them to achieve the targets set. Imposed budgets would not have the same effect
- facilitate the co-ordination of all aspects of a business

- highlight present weaknesses such as unauthorized overspending, or lack of and waste of resources
- can be compared with actual performance. Comparison with last year's activity is not so meaningful
- can be used to establish transfer prices for charging internal services such as maintenance and computer time.

Behavioural aspects of budgetary control

Whilst the previous paragraph outlined the nature and usefulness of a system of budgetary control, and the remainder of this chapter will spell out more procedural details, it must never be forgotten that organizations are comprised of people, not just targets of performance. We must therefore take account of human attitudes and behaviour. A well-designed system, operated in conditions of low employee morale, may not be as effective as a less sophisticated system operated by highly motivated employees.

Participation in setting budgets

Goals imposed by management are usually resented by supervisors; they may be counterproductive and lead to a dampening of motivation and initiative. The undesirable aspects of budgeting systems will then tend to surface, such as:

- the spending of all budget allowances, even when not needed
- switching expenditure from over- to under-spent jobs, to hide unauthorized expenditure
- shoddy work

- deferral of essential expenditure, such as maintenance
- concentration on short-term performance to the detriment of long-term aims
- complying with budget even though higher achievement might have been possible.

On the other hand, participation in budget setting should be real, not just a formal exercise. Managers should be given a real measure of self-control and their goals should be common with the goals of the organization. High morale is implicit in effective participation.

The extent of participation will vary with the type of organization and will range from complete autonomy granted to divisional investment-centre managers, to a more authoritarian style where operations are repetitive and easily understood.

Attainable standards

Real participation requires that the method of deriving targets of performance is understood and can be influenced by those affected. Goals must be legitimate and attainable, because, if they are fairly set, they will be adopted as personal levels of aspiration. Most managers will strive to better fairly set high targets; conversely, performance will deteriorate if they are set either at an unattainably high level or at too low a level.

Success in achieving agreed budget goals generally leads to a raising of managers' aspiration levels; failure to a lowering.

Managers should be held responsible for activities, costs, etc., that they can control. For example, head office costs may be apportioned to a division, but they should be labelled in the divisional operating report as 'uncontrollable'.

'Freedom to fail' should exist, otherwise managers will never deviate from the short-term plan, even when conditions are dictating that they ought to do so from a long-term viewpoint.

Performance measurement

Feedback of performance information to managers ought to be viewed constructively. Responsibility should not be equated with 'blame', quite the contrary. Measurements should ideally be linked with a system of rewards, which might include promotion or simply gratitude for a job well done.

Information feedback should be frequent, to enable managers to take effective corrective action, and should be 'flexed' to accord with changing operational conditions.

Though performance measures tend to be expressed in quantitative terms, qualitative evaluations of customer service, employee welfare and comparison with competitors, may be more effective in their impact on morale.

Budget administration

Budgeting procedure will vary from the relatively simple to the complex, depending upon the size and nature of the activity carried out by an organization. In a one-man business, planning may be nonexistent, or at best consist of simple cash control. At the other extreme, in a large enterprise, budgetary control will be a formalized procedure, headed by a budget officer, guided by a budget committee and specified in a budget manual.

The budget committee will probably include the managing director, the budget officer, who may be the management accountant, and all the functional executives. Its main role is to:

- reconcile differences between the managers responsible for producing the component parts of the budget
- ensure that the forecasts are within the framework set by the long-term plan
- co-ordinate and consolidate the budget
- present the budget to the board of directors for their approval and communication to responsible managers
- review the budgets in the light of actual performance and recommend necessary revisions.

The budget officer is responsible for producing and updating a budget manual which makes provision for:

- a specification of all the budgets to be prepared, indicating who is responsible for each
- a timetable specifying the latest date for the submission of each budget to the budget committee
- guidance on the procedure, principles, assumptions, constraints, policies and the documentation to be used in the preparation of each budget.

Outline of a system of budgetary control

Figure 19 charts each of the steps in the preparation of a complete system of budgets. Each of the steps is briefly described below, but in Chapter 13 the component budgets are illustrated and examined in more detail.

1 *Long-term policy*. Profit and other objectives are agreed, and strategic decisions are made to achieve those objectives.
2 *Implementation*. Of financial, investment and marketing strategic decisions.
3 *Short-term forecasts*. Of sales, production and associated costs.

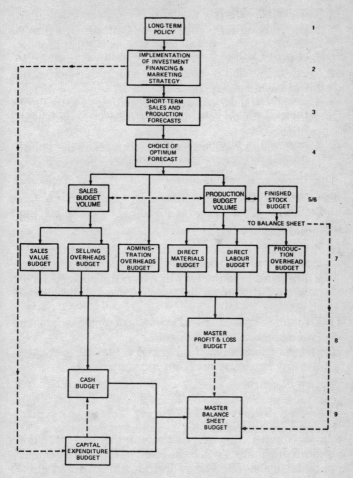

Figure 19. Outline budgetary control system

4 *Choice of optimum forecast.* From the alternatives presented in **3**, with short-term limiting factors mainly influencing this decision.

5/6 *Sales and production volume budgets.* Reconciled after taking account of any factors limiting the firm's ability to produce or sell, and also existing and planned stock levels.

7 *Sales revenue and cost budgets.* Natural derivatives of the sales and production budgets.

8 *Master profit and loss budget.* Consolidates the totals of sales revenue and cost budgets to arrive at budgeted profit.

9 *Master balance sheet budget.* Consolidates all the financial budgets, comprising debtors, creditors, stocks, cash and capital expenditure.

A further two steps that are not shown on the budget flow chart are worth adding to complete the planning and control cycle:

10 *Actual sales and costs recorded in the management accounting system, and presentation of periodic results.* In a form similar to the way in which the budgets have been prepared, to facilitate comparison at the control stage.

11 *Recording, explaining and acting on variations between budgeted and actual performance.*

12 *Budgets reviewed.* In the light of actual performance and any necessary revisions recommended.

The budgeting starting point

Before commencing preparation of the budgets, the various contributors will be advised of top-management policy changes. These may include the planned cessation of some activities, significant reorganizations within production centres and changes in marketing strategy – including price amendments. Assumptions regarding inflation, wage increases and forecast fiscal changes, such as increased VAT, will be advised, together with any known limitations on the volume of production or sales during the coming budget period.

Subject to these overall policy dictates, an initial condensed form of profit and loss forecast will be produced. Sales revenue is forecast first, then direct materials, direct labour and variable overhead are deducted as assumed percentages of sales; fixed costs are then deducted to give a first profit forecast. Other forecasts will follow, with limiting factors taken into account and perhaps overcome, by planned overtime, extra shift working or subcontracting, until the most acceptable forecast is produced and approved.

Points to note in budgeting costs

A common practice in budgeting costs is to take last year's costs and add a percentage for inflation as the budget for the coming year. This may be an acceptable procedure in very small firms, where very little is changing from year to year, but it can be a totally misleading and dangerous practice: last year's activity may be higher or lower than forecast for next year; costs may be changing at rates different from inflation; and there may also be a false assumption that the equipment, methods and efficiency attained previously will be continued. Further, if managers are allowed to decide the added increment to last year's costs, they will tend to build in 'slack' sufficient to enable them to achieve or to better their budgets. 'Parkinson's law' will ensure that they are euqally as capable of achieving a loosely set as a tightly set budget.

Zero-based budgeting attempts to solve this problem of slack budgets by requiring managers to justify their existing levels of operation, together with their associated costs, on the assumption that they are commencing operations from 'scratch'.

The separate activities of each department are identi-fied and have to be justified in terms of costs and bene-fits. Each activity is viewed as a decision package to be evaluated and ranked, together with alternative or addi-tional decision packages. Essential activities will be given priority, subject to cost limitations, and then other activities added, subject to the upper spending limit.

The zero-based technique is certainly superior to the 'add a bit on for luck' approach. It is more penetrating, invokes the concept of 'value for money' and motivates the more able managers. Its drawbacks are its cost and the lengthy review time required; but these can be smoothed out by reviewing each budget centre, say once every three to five years.

The technique is particularly applicable to service departments and in the appraisal of production over-heads, and also in public sector organizations, such as local authorities, where engineered costs (i.e. using method and work study) are difficult to apply.

Setting standard costs

The standard cost of a product is what it *should* cost to produce under *currently attainable conditions*. This implies a careful assessment of the quantities and prices of all the resources combining to create each product.

Standard costs are most applicable in industries where products and processes are standardized; when there is only one product and production processes are continuous, for example. They apply naturally to food processing, cosmetics and cement production. But where work is non-repetitive, for example in jobbing industries such as motor maintenance, standards may only be applicable to routine jobs.

Setting standards for direct materials

The standard quantity of materials and components incorporated into a product is relatively easily ascertained from the product specification; it being presumed that the product design and quality meets the requirements of the customer. Allowance should be made in the standard for normal losses in production due to evaporation, chemical action, etc.

Standard prices will be those expected to apply during the budget period. Past prices being irrelevant, unless they remain unchanged. The purchasing manager is responsible for negotiating best prices, therefore he sets the standard price for each material. Rapid inflation can soon render standard prices out of date and if this happens, arrangements should be made to review standards during the budget period.

Setting standards for direct labour

If an incentive payment scheme is already in existence, a work study engineer will already have specified standard working conditions for each job and the grade of labour required. Using scientific techniques of observation, he will have analysed the work content of each operation, making due allowances for the personal and ergonomic needs of workers, and have established times for all the operations necessary to complete each product.

Should work study not have been introduced, past experience could initially be the best guide to setting standard times, subject to rigorous reappraisal in due course.

Wage rates will already be established by agreement with unions or other employee representatives, but where differential rates are paid for merit awards and long service, standard rates for each grade of labour will be weighted averages of the different rates paid. Wage increases that can be foreseen should also be included in the standard.

The standard cost of labour for each product, then, is simply the total of standard labour hours multiplied by standard rate for each operation.

Setting standards for overhead

Recall from Chapter 7 how overhead is charged to production by using predetermined overhead rates. Each rate is calculated by dividing a forecast activity level for each cost centre into the forecast cost at that level of output. Standard overhead rates are calculated in much the same way.

Each expense head should be analysed as to its behaviour (using one of the methods discussed in Chapter 8), but with the emphasis on *what the cost should be*, not what it has been in the past. The variable and fixed overhead-cost rates are then determined by dividing the total of those heads of cost by the budgeted level of output – usually expressed in labour or machine hours.

The major problem in the above calculations is choice of budgeted level of output, Figure 20 showing the alternative activity levels that one might adopt.

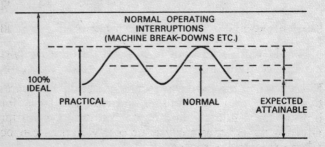

Figure 20. Alternative standard activity levels

Ideal, at 100% activity, is unrealistic in the majority of firms, and overhead rates calculated on this basis would almost certainly lead to under-recovery of overheads, as well as frustrating production supervisors who are unable to achieve the 'ideal' output level.

Practical level (say 85%), may be realistic in firms or cost centres where full-capacity working is the 'norm', but when production fluctuates from year to year, *expected attainable* may be a more realistic basis for control purposes. This is calculated on the forecast activity for the coming year.

Normal level of activity is based upon long-term expectations to make and sell and takes into account the cyclical nature of the market – some years demand being high, and in other years low. This is the level chosen by many firms because using the same activity base each year values stock consistently and selling price quotations can benefit from the stability of the normal rate.

The standard cost of a product may be summarized as follows:

Standard material A 3 units	@ £2 per unit	£6	
B 2 units	@ £1 per unit	2	£8
Standard labour – Cutting 3 hrs	@ £2 per hour	£6	
– Welding 2 hrs	@ £3 per hour	£6	
– Finishing 1 hr	@ £3 per hour	£3	15
Standard overhead	6 hrs @ £3 per hour		18
			£41

Knowledge of standard costs will make budget preparation easier, and, in addition, provide the basis for introducing a full standard cost-accounting system for which a penetrating analysis of cost variances can be made for control purposes.

13 Budgeting – A Complete Illustration

H. A. Products Ltd is a subsidiary company of Hemming Agricultural Machinery Ltd. It was established two years ago to manufacture and supply containers to the parent company, but it has since developed an outside market which takes at least 50% of its output.

The company's current financial position is disclosed in the following balance sheet:

H. A. Products Ltd
Balance sheet at 31 December 19–1

£000s

Fixed assets:

| Plant and machinery (cost) | 400 | |
| less depreciation | 40 | 360 |

| Motor vehicles (cost) | 100 | |
| less depreciation | 20 | 80 |

440

Current assets:

Cash	92	
Stock – finished goods	38	
– work in progress	60	
– materials	80	
Debtors	120	

390

less current liabilities:

| Creditors | 30 | 360 |

£800

Financed by:

| Ordinary share capital | 600 |
| Profit and loss account | 200 |

£800

NOTES:

1 Amounts receivable from debtors will be paid in January 19–2.
2 Amounts owing to creditors will be paid in January 19–2.
3 All stocks are valued at the standard costs given below.

4 It is assumed that work in progress will be the same value at the end of year 19–2.
5 Cash (£92,480) and finished goods (£37,520) are shown above to the nearest £000s for simplicity.
6 Debtors and creditors outstanding at 31 December 19–2 are £155,000 and £38,000 respectively.

The following sales information relates to the year just ended, i.e. 19–1.

| Product | Quantity in units | | Selling price per unit £ | Year end stock (units) |
	Internal	External		
Container A	1,000	900	270	100
Container B	800	900	180	80
Container C	320	400	230	60

Sales to external customers are forecast to double next year and the parent company will require a 25% increase in all models. Capacity has already been installed to cope with the increased production requirements. Sales prices are to be increased to £300, £200 and £250 for A, B and C respectively, and it is also planned to increase finished stocks to 200, 180 and 160 respectively by the end of 19–2. The parent company is charged the same selling prices as external customers.

The *standard direct material and labour specifications* for each product are as follows:

	A	B	C
Material P – units	10	6	7
Material Q – units	6	3	5
Labour hours – cut and press	12	8	8
Labour hours – finishing	11	6	8

Standard material and labour costs are:

Material P	£4 a unit
Material Q	£5 a unit
Labour – cut and press	£5 a unit
Labour – finishing	£4 a unit

Direct material stocks at 31 December 19–1 were:

Material P	12,500 units @ £4 =	£50,000
Material Q	6,000 units @ £5 =	30,000
		£80,000

per balance sheet 31/12/19–1

The planned stocks of material for the end of 19–2 are:
Material P 15,000 units
Material Q 8,000 units

With the aid of the above and further information, the management accountant is now required to co-ordinate the preparation of a complete set of budgets.

Sales budget

The sales budget is the responsibility of the sales manager and in most firms is the keystone upon which all other budgets are built. It will be prepared after the optimum forecast for the year has been agreed, and will therefore have taken account of production and other limiting factors.

Its preparation will probably rely on information from one or all of the following sources:

1 *The analysing and extrapolation of sales trends* – particularly of a seasonal or cyclical nature, using statistical techniques of forecasting, knowledge of industry growth, competition and general trade prospects, planned sales-promotion expenditure, forecasts of National Income, VAT and interest rates.
2 *Estimates by own field staff* – sales representatives have a unique knowledge and 'feel' for their own sales areas, that head office staff will not possess, especially when judging the future demand for new products. In this respect, certain areas may be chosen for field tests for new products.
3 *Market research* – by own staff or consultants who

advise on probable product demand and market
share, after taking account of promotional policy and
possible competitors' reactions.

Based upon last year's figures, but adjusted for expected
increases, the sales budget would appear as follows:

BUDGET 1

H. A. Products Ltd
Sales budget for the year to 31 December 19–2

| Container | Sales in units | | Total | Sales price | Value |
	Internal	External		£	£
A	1,250	1,800	3,050	300	915,000
B	1,000	1,800	2,800	200	560,000
C	400	800	1,200	250	300,000
					1,775,000

Most businesses require a more detailed analysis and
build-up of projected sales than is given above. Sales in
home and export markets, and by area, representative
and channel of distribution, will provide more information upon which realistic budgets can be set, and ultimately monitored.

Note that prices and volume have been increased as
required. CVP analysis must have assured the company
that the market could stand the price increase. As
regards internal sales, management must ensure that
parent company sales are not compromised by un-
reasonably set transfer prices.

Production budget (volume)

As the production manager will ultimately be held
responsible for achieving production targets, he should
play the major role in compiling the production budget.

The long-range plans of H. A. Products will have

already ensured that the necessary machinery and other resources are in place to provide the increase in output scheduled for 19–2. The production budget for the coming year is given below:

BUDGET 2

H. A. Products Limited
Production budget for the year to 31 December 19–2

	A	B	C
	---------- units ----------		
Sales budget	3,050	2,800	1,200
less opening stock	(100)	(80)	(60)
add closing stock	200	180	160
Production required	3,150	2,900	1,300

Direct labour budget

Assuming that standard production times have been established for each product by work-study techniques (see Chapter 12), the direct labour hours required to satisfy the production budget is found by multiplying production quantities by the standard hours per product. It follows that the number of employees required for each department is budgeted total-labour hours divided by hours in a normal working week.

The above calculations will reveal whether more employees have to be engaged, or whether there is surplus labour. If the latter, management will be obliged to declare its policy. If the employees are skilled, a decision to retain them is likely, because, once released, they may never return, even though there may be work for them in the future. If they are retained, their wages cost will be treated as an indirect expense.

A further factor to recognize is that automation has

considerably reduced the number of direct operatives required in manufacturing operations. The labour-intensive days are over and direct employees are more and more becoming 'machine minders', who will be required whether or not production is flowing. In these circumstances, direct labour is virtually a fixed cost and does not vary in direct proportion to output as is usually supposed.

By reference to the production budget (for product volume), and the standard times and rates given at the beginning of the chapter, the direct labour budget can be compiled:

BUDGET 3

H. A. Products Limited
Direct labour budget for the year 19–2

Product	Budgeted output units	Hours per unit C&P	fin.	Total hours C&P	fin.
A	3,150	12	11	37,800	34,650
B	2,900	8	6	23,200	17,400
C	1,300	8	8	10,400	10,400
				71,400	62,450
Standard rate per hour				£5	£4
Budgeted labour cost				£357,000	£249,800

Direct materials usage budget

Although the control of direct material is the responsibility of production department supervisors, the quantity budget will invariably be scheduled by the purchasing manager. Indeed, the computer is admirably suited to calculating and printing the required information by reference to the production volume budget and product specifications.

The figures for our example are as shown below:

BUDGET 4

H. A. Products Limited
Direct materials usage budget for the year 19–2

Product	Budgeted output	Quantity per unit		Total units required	
		P	Q	P	Q
A	3,150	10	6	31,500	18,900
B	2,900	6	3	17,400	8,700
C	1,300	7	5	9,100	6,500
				58,000	34,100
Standard price per unit				£4	£5
Standard material usage cost				£232,000	£170,500

Direct materials purchase budget

The purchasing manager is responsible for the procurement of direct materials and other supplies, and his direct materials cost budget will take account of production requirements, planned prices, stocks of material held at present and planned for the end of the budget period. In large multi-product organizations, the role of the purchasing manager is complicated and onerous: he has to be knowledgeable about current sources of materials, as well as possible substitutes for them; he should aim to buy at the keenest prices consistent with quality; and be skilled in negotiating purchase contracts.

The purchase budget follows from the usage budget – adjusted for opening and closing stocks of raw materials:

BUDGET 5

H. A. Products Limited
Direct materials purchase budget for the year 19–2

	P	Q
	------ *units* ------	
Production requirement	58,000	34,100
add closing stock	15,000	8,000
less opening stock	(12,500)	(6,000)
	60,500	36,100
Standard prices	£4	£5
Total purchase budget	£242,000	£180,500

Production overhead budgets

An overhead budget is produced for each production department by the responsible supervisor, having regard to the output requirements of his production budget and any anticipated changes, in prices or additional depreciation for example. To keep this exercise simple, however, only a total overhead budget will be scheduled.

BUDGET 6

H. A. Products Limited
Production overhead budget for the year 19–2

	Fixed £	Variable £
Controllable costs:		
Supervision	19,956	
Indirect labour		20,000
Indirect materials		17,344
Electric power		9,550
Maintenance		8,000
Tools		4,000
Non-controllable costs:		
Depreciation	40,000	
Rent and rates	15,000	
	74,956	58,894
Budgeted hours worked	133,850	133,850
Standard overhead rates	£0.56	£0.44

NOTES:

1 Controllable costs are grouped separately to indicate those expenses which are the direct responsibility of the appropriate supervisor, because he can positively influence the amount.

2 Separate fixed and variable rates are calculated to facilitate variance analysis (see Chapter 14) and to 'flex' the budget to actual output attained, for control purposes.

3 Although some expenses would be a mixture of fixed and variable cost behaviour, this again has been ignored for the sake of simplicity.

4 It is assumed that direct labour hours is the major variable influencing variable costs.

Standard product manufacturing cost

Product standard costing data given at the beginning of
this chapter, has already been drawn upon to compile
the direct materials and direct labour budgets. In this
section we bring together the same data, together with
production overhead, to determine standard product
cost.

This information is useful, not only to value stocks for
budget and control purposes, but also to feed relevant
costs into the decision-making process.

	Standard price £	A £		B £		C £	
Material							
P	4 ⎱ per	10 = 40		6 = 24		7 = 28	
Q	5 ⎰ unit	6 = 30	70	3 = 15	39	5 = 25	53
Labour							
C&P	5 ⎱ per	12 = 60		8 = 40		8 = 40	
Fin.	4 ⎰ hour	11 = 44	104	6 = 24	64	8 = 32	72
Overhead	1 per hour	23 =	23	14 =	14	16 =	16
Standard product cost			£197		£117		£141

NOTE:

The standard overhead rate of £1 per hour is the total of
the fixed and variable rates shown in the production
overhead budget section.

Selling and administration overhead budget

This budget is the sales manager's responsibility. It will
contain a large element of fixed costs, most of them

discretionary but some of them committed. The salaries of field representatives will depend upon management policy relating to area coverage, and can be increased or decreased at the discretion of management. Whereas a three-year contract with an advertising agency is a committed cost.

The major variable costs are sales commission (4% of sales value in this company) and some distribution costs, both of which will be directly related to sales, not production.

BUDGET 7

H. A. Products Limited
Selling and administration overhead budget for the year 19–2

	£
Salaries	30,000
Sales commission	71,000
Depreciation	10,000
Distribution	17,750
Other expenses	21,250
	£150,000

Budgeted Profit and Loss Account

This statement, together with the cash budget and budgeted balance sheet, are the master budget summaries which must gain the approval of the budget committee before their release, as the definitive plan for the year.

Recall that the profit and loss account does not measure receipts and payments – that is the province of the cash budget. The total sales for a period, whether for goods or services, may include sales for which customers have not yet paid. Conversely, the cost of materials used is in the profit and loss budget, even though some of it is not paid for by the period end. Indeed, some of the material would have been in stock at the beginning of the period, but may have been paid for in a previous period.

BUDGET 8

H. A. Products Limited
Budgeted profit and loss account for the year 19–2

		£
Sales (Budget 1)		1,775,000
Cost of goods sold:		
direct materials (Budget 4)	402,500	
direct labour (Budget 3)	606,800	
production overhead (Budget 6)	133,850	
	1,143,150	
Add opening work in progress	60,000	
Less closing work in progress	(60,000)	
Cost of production	1,143,150	
add opening finished goods (Note 2)	37,520	
less closing finished goods (Note 2)	(83,020)	
Cost of goods sold		1,097,650
Gross profit		677,350
Selling and admin. overhead (Budget 7)		150,000
Net profit		£527,350

NOTES:

1 It is assumed that work in progress is the same value at the beginning and end of the year.
2 Opening and closing finished stocks are valued as follows:

	Opening stocks units	Closing stocks units	Standard cost per unit £	Total standard cost Opening £	Closing £
A	100	200	197	19,700	39,400
B	80	180	117	9,360	21,060
C	60	160	141	8,460	22,560
				£37,520	£83,020

3 Alternatively, cost of sales can be shown in a shortened form as the product of unit sales and unit standard cost; the above presentation is used to enable one to check the cost of sales back to the constituent cost budgets (see budget references).

Cash budget

Cash is the 'lubricant' without which businesses would grind to a halt. Financial provision for the expansion taking place in H. A. Products' operations was probably part of the company's strategic planning a year or more ago. In the short term, however, there may be temporary shortages of cash to bridge, or surpluses to invest temporarily, and a cash budget can reveal these conditions.

It is compiled by drawing information from the operational budgets, but takes into account other receipts and payments not reflected in those budgets. These include:

■ capital receipts from loans and share issues
■ sales of surplus fixed assets, such as land and buildings
■ payment of taxation to the Inland Revenue and dividends to shareholders
■ purchase of assets such as machines, motor vehicles and buildings (these would normally be scheduled in a capital expenditure budget, which

has not been produced in this exercise as all fixed asset additions took place last year).

The most important aspect in the construction of a cash budget is to ensure that it reflects the actual timing of cash flows. Cash payments do not necessarily coincide with either the receipt or the use of a resource. For example, material may be received in January, not paid for until February and not used until March. Again, goods may be sold in April and recorded as sales in that month, but not paid for by the customer until May. A machine purchased and wholly paid for in October will be used over many years; its payment will be shown in October, but its depreciation will be an annual charge in the profit and loss account during its useful life.

Whilst the budget would normally be broken down into monthly or four-weekly periods, H. A. Products' budget is shown below in summary form for simplicity:

BUDGET 9

H. A. Products Limited
Cash budget for the year 19–2

		£
Receipts:		
Sales (Budget 1)	1,775,000	
Add opening debtors	120,000	
	1,895,000	
Less closing debtors	155,000	1,740,000
Payments:		
Purchase of materials (Budget 5)	422,500	
Add opening creditors	30,000	
	452,500	
Less closing creditors	38,000	414,500
Direct wages (Budget 3)		606,800
Production overhead (Budget 6)		93,850
Selling and admin. overhead (Budget 7)		140,000
		1,255,150
Surplus for the year		484,850
Add opening balance		92,480
Closing cash balance		£ 577,330

NOTES:

1 It is assumed that there are no debtors or creditors for overheads.
2 Depreciation is included in both production, and selling and administration budgets as an expense, but is not a cash item for inclusion above.

Master balance sheet budget

H. A. Products' financial position at the beginning of the budget year is shown in the balance sheet at the beginning of this chapter. Changes in that position will take place as the result of transactions planned in the several budgets, and these culminate in a revised financial position as shown in the budgeted balance sheet below.

BUDGET 10

H. A. Products Limited
Budgeted balance sheet for the year 19–2

Fixed assets:	Cost £	Depreciation £	Net £
Plant and machinery	400,000	80,000	320,000
Motor vehicles	100,000	30,000	70,000
	500,000	110,000	390,000
Current assets:			
Cash (Budget 9)		577,330	
Stocks:			
finished goods		83,020	
work in progress		60,000	
materials		100,000	
Debtors		155,000	
		975,350	
less current liabilities:			
Creditors		38,000	937,350
			£1,327,350
Financed by:			
Ordinary share capital			600,000
Profit and loss account:			
Opening balance		200,000	
Profit for the year (Budget 8)		527,350	727,350
			£1,327,350

14   Budget Variance Analysis

WHAT ARE VARIANCES?

The final stage in the management process depicted in Figure 2, Chapter 1, is 'control', which implies monitoring the progress of plans after implementation and taking necessary action either to correct deviations or to change plans. Controlling and planning are therefore inextricably linked, because action stems out of decision-taking.

The decisions to be made will depend upon the feedback from the management information system, a major part of which is provided by the management accountant, who produces regular management reports for departmental managers. These reports will compare actual operational performance with budget, differences being shown as variances.

If a formalized standard costing system is in operation, variances will be automatically recorded in the accounting system as they occur, but reporting of budget variances can take place without such a formalized system.

Variance analysis reports upon:

- each of the elements of cost and revenue, i.e. material, labour, overhead and sales
- whether prices paid for resources or received from sales are more or less than planned
- whether quantities of resources used or sales volumes are more or less than planned
- what *has* happened, compared with what *should have* happened. In this respect, budget allowances

are *'flexed'*, i.e. adjusted to relate to the actual
activity achieved

■ the performance of each separate responsibility
centre.

This chapter demonstrates how variances are calculated
and presented to management. For illustration purposes, the standard costs and budgets of H. A. Products
Ltd featured in Chapter 13 are drawn upon, and compared with the company's actual performance for the
year 19–2 as follows:

Sales for the year:

Container	Selling price £	Sales in units Internal	External
A	280	1,500	1,700
B	200	1,000	1,800
C	240	400	700

Production for the year:

Container	Units	Time taken Direct Labour hours C&P	Fin.
A	3,250	39,800	35,500
B	2,900	23,200	17,500
C	1,300	10,600	10,100

Direct labour rates paid for the year averaged £5.30 and
£4.20 per hour for the C&P and Fin. departments
respectively.

Direct Materials:

Material	Actual usage units	Actual purchases units	
P	60,000	61,000	@ £4.10 per unit
Q	35,200	36,000	@ £5.20 per unit

Production Overhead:

Fixed overhead totalled £76,000 for the year.
Variable overhead totalled £61,000 for the year.

Selling and Administration Overhead:

This was £151,500 for the year, including 4% commission on actual sales value.

Guidelines for the Calculation of all Cost Variances:

1 Two basic variances are calculated for each cost element – *price* and *quantity*.
2 Each variance is calculated by deducting *actual* from *standard* cost.
3 Variances are either *adverse* (A) or *favourable* (F) according to whether actual is more or less than standard cost respectively.
4 We compare the actual with the standard cost of *what did happen* – not *what is planned to happen* – in the budget.

DIRECT MATERIAL VARIANCES

Price Variances:

Note that the quantity purchased is not necessarily the same as the quantity used (see below). Price variances are best extracted when the invoice for materials is received, because stocks are then recorded at standard cost and the variances are reported to management at the time they occur, not when the material is used.

(standard price – actual price) × quantity purchased = variance

P (4.00 – 4.10) 61,000 = 6,100 (A)
Q (5.00 – 5.20) 36,000 = 7,200 (A) = £13,300 (A)

Possible explanations:
(a) unforeseen increases in suppliers' prices; (b) inefficient buying, i.e. quantity discounts not negotiated, rush orders; (c) change of supplier; (d) better than standard quality bought; (e) planning error.

Usage Variance:

(Standard usage for containers produced – actual usage) × standard price = variance

   units   *units*
P (59,000 – 60,000) 4 = 4,000 (A)
Q (34,700 – 35,200) 5 = 2,500 (A) = £6,500 (A)

Standard Usage:

P (3,250 × 10) + (2,900 × 6) + (1,300 × 7) = 59,000
Q (3,250 × 6) + (2,900 × 3) + (1,300 × 5) = 34,700

Possible explanations:
(a) more than normal scrapped material; (b) use of inferior material; (c) use of non-standard labour or machines; (d) lack of supervision; (e) machine or operator inefficiency; (f) planning error.

DIRECT LABOUR VARIANCES

Rate of Pay Variance:

(Standard rate – actual rate paid) × hours worked = variance

C&P (5.00 – 5.30) 73,600 = 22,080 (A)
Fin. (4.00 – 4.20) 63,100 = 12,620 (A) = £34,700 (A)

Possible explanations:
(a) unforeseen increases; (b) use of non-standard labour, i.e. high instead of low skilled; (c) planning error.

Labour Efficiency Variance

(Standard hours produced – actual hours worked) × standard rate = variance

NOTE:

Standard hours represents the time that should have been taken to complete actual production.

C&P (*72,600 – 73,600) 5 = 5,000 (A)
Fin. (*63,550 – 63,100) 4 = 1,800 (F) = 3,200 (A)

*Standard hours:

C&P (3,250 × 12) + (2,900 × 8) + (1,300 × 8) = 72,600
Fin. (3,250 × 11) + (2,900 × 6) + (1,300 × 8) = 63,550

Possible explanations:
(a) low productivity; (b) use of non-standard employees, machines, methods or conditions; (c) poor supervision; (d) planning error for adverse variance.

The actual hours worked relate to *productive* time only. Any idle time of direct workers, whether planned or unforeseen (perhaps resulting from management policy to retain skilled labour), will be charged to production overheads. The resultant element of indirect labour not budgeted will be revealed as a variance in the production overhead schedule.

Production Overhead Variances

Variable Overhead Expenditure Variance

(Hours worked × standard variable overhead rate) − actual variable cost

Recall that variable overhead varies with direct labour hours worked @ £0.44 per hour.

$$(136,700 \times 0.44) - 61,000$$
$$60,148 - 61,000 = £852 \text{ (A)}$$

Possible explanations:
(a) unforeseen cost increase; (b) inefficient usage; (c) planning error.
 Detailed examination of individual expenses is required to fully explain this variance.

Variable Overhead Efficiency Variance

(Standard hours produced − actual hours worked) × variable overhead rate

$$(136,150 - 136,700) \ £0.44 = £242 \text{ (A)}$$

Possible explanations:
As this variance is directly related to labour efficiency, the reasons given for the latter are the same for variable overhead.

Fixed Overhead Expenditure Variance

(budgeted cost – actual cost)

(74,956 – 76,000) = £1,044 (A)

Possible explanations:
An examination of the individual items comprising the fixed overhead total will reveal those that have over and underspent.

Fixed Overhead Capacity Variance

This variance arises because more or less hours than budgeted were available for productive use. Here we look back at the *original* budget, to measure the cost of losing or gaining capacity.

(Standard capacity hours – actual hours worked) × standard fixed overhead rate

(133,850 – 136,700) × £0.56 = £1,596 (F)

Possible explanations: (if variance was *adverse*)
(a) industrial action; (b) shortage of labour; (c) illness; (d) unexpected national holiday; (e) machine breakdown; (f) non-delivery of machines; (g) reduced sales; (h) poor supervision; (i) planning error. However, the favourable variance indicates more capacity than planned.

Fixed Overhead Efficiency Variance

This measures a further gain or loss because more or less hours were produced than were made available for productive use. Note the direct connection with labour efficiency.

(Standard hours produced – actual hours worked) × standard fixed overhead rate

(136,150 – 136,700) × £0.56 = £308 (A)

All the overhead variances can be checked in total as follows:

(Standard overhead absorbed – actual total overhead cost)

NOTE:

Standard overhead absorbed = standard hours produced × 1 = £136,150
(136,150 – 137,000) = £850 (A)

Selling and Administration Overhead Variances:

The total variance is the difference between budgeted and actual cost, i.e. £150,000 – 151,500 = £1,500 (A); but a more detailed analysis of individual expense variances is required.

Sales Variances

We still keep the spotlight on *price* and *quantity* here. Have we received more or less than standard prices for product sales? Have we sold more or less in volume than budgeted?

Note, however, that as regards sales volume, we do refer to the *original* budget. Recall that in the calculation of cost variances we '*flexed*' the budget to obtain a more realistic yardstick against which to compare actual cost.

A further point to note is that *sales volume variance* is measured in the number of profit margins lost or gained. As our objective is to show why the actual and budgeted profits differ, lost sales affects profit only. The goods that might have been sold are not lost – they are still in stock, and all that has been lost on them is their profit. In the following period, these goods will most likely be sold and their profit reflected in the accounts for that period.

Sales Price Variance:

(Standard price – actual price) × quantity sold

A (300 – 280) 3,200 = 64,000 (A)
B (200 – 200) 2,800 =   –
C (250 – 240) 1,100 = 11,000 (A) = £75,000 (A)

Possible explanations:
(a) competition forcing price cuts to stimulate sales; (b) lower costs allowing prices to be reduced (though lower costs are conspicuous by their absence in this exercise).

Sales Volume Variance:

(Budgeted volume – actual volume) × standard profit per unit

A (3,050 – 3,200) 103 = 15,450 (F)
B (2,800 – 2,800)   83 =   –
C (1,200 – 1,100) 109 = 10,900 (A) = £4,550 (F)

Standard profit per unit is calculated by deducting standard manufacturing cost from standard selling price, viz:

A (300 – 197); B (200 – 117); C (250 – 141)

Possible explanations:
(a) competitive pressure on external sales of C; (b) additional capacity (see fixed overhead capacity variance) enabled us to sell more of A.

Reconciling actual with budgeted profit

Presented in orthodox form, the profit of H. A. Products Ltd for 19–2 is as follows:

H. A. Products Limited
Profit and loss account for the year 19–2

	Quantity	Selling price		Product sales	Total
	units	£		£	£
Sales A	3,200	280	=	896,000	
B	2,800	200	=	560,000	
C	1,100	240	=	264,000	1,720,000

less cost of sales:		
Direct materials stock 1 Jan.	80,000	
purchased	437,300	
	517,300	
stock 31 Dec.	(88,000)	
Cost of materials used	429,300	
Direct labour	655,100	
Production overhead	137,000	
Cost of production	1,221,400	
Add opening finished goods	37,520	
Less closing finished goods	(87,270)	
Cost of goods sold		1,171,650
Gross profit		548,350
Selling and admin. overhead		151,500
Actual net profit		£396,850

In order to highlight the differences between the actual profit shown above and the planned profit, an abbreviated summary of budgeted net profit, adjusted for the sales and cost variances calculated earlier in this chapter, is produced below. This variance profit and loss account, together with an explanatory memorandum, will be submitted to top management.

Variance profit and loss account for the year 19–2

		£
Budgeted net profit		527,350
Sales variances:		
price	75,000 (A)	
quantity	4,550 (F)	70,450 (A)
		456,900
Production variances:		
Direct material – price	13,300 (A)	
Direct material – usage	6,500 (A)	
Direct labour – rate	34,700 (A)	
Direct labour efficiency	3,200 (A)	
Variable overhead – expenditure	852 (A)	
Fixed overhead – expenditure	1,044 (A)	
Variable overhead – efficiency	242 (A)	
Fixed overhead – efficiency	308 (A)	
Fixed overhead – capacity	1,596 (F)	58,550 (A)
		398,350
Selling and administration expenditure	1,500 (A)	1,500 (A)
Actual net profit		£396,850

15   Informing Management

Need for action

When your temperature is high you know there is *something* wrong with you, but you do not know *what*. Further diagnosis by your doctor is needed to find the root cause of your feeling unwell, and only when he has this information can he prescribe treatment to put you on the road to recovery.

Business managers are in much the same position as the doctor. Performance reports by way of budget and actual comparisons, and standard costing variance measurements, quantify deviations from plan, but they need explanatory support. Only then can management take appropriate corrective action to:

- bring short-term plans back on course
- modify short-term plans in the light of changing circumstances
- review and amend long-term plans if circumstances dictate.

Responsibility for action

Who takes the necessary action depends on the structure of management in a business and the extent to which responsibility is delegated. An organization chart, such as that depicted in Figure 1, Chapter 1, is a starting point, but duties and responsibilities need to be spelt out more specifically in budgeting and other procedure manuals, and on a personal level, in each manager's job specification.

The essential criterion of responsibility is the ability to *influence* a particular result. You will recall that this was pointed up in the form of the production overhead budget in Chapter 13, where budgeted expenses were separated according to whether they were '*controllable*' or '*uncontrollable*' by the production manager. The concept of influence is not so precise as control, but is more pertinent because it covers the grey areas of cost which may be influenced by more than one manager.

For example, maintenance of machinery is the prime responsibility of the maintenance department manager, but if the manager of the production department whose machinery is being maintained does not exert some influence over the time taken in repairing his machines, his production targets will suffer. For this reason, he will express his concern if his machines are out of action for an unreasonable time, even though he does not directly supervise maintenance engineers.

The extent of each manager's responsibility varies in relation to the size and type of organization, but using Figure 1 as a model, each of the departments reporting to the finance, marketing, production and research and development functional mangers, can be classified as *cost centres*, each under the control of its own manager. Cost centres are areas of responsibility in respect of which costs are accumulated, compared with budgets and reported back to the controlling manager.

At the *functional* level, the information reported to the finance, marketing, production, and research and development managers will summarize the operations of the cost centres under their control; whilst the *managing director* will receive overall summarized statements of costs, profit, return on investment and other information, relevant to his planning role.

In much larger organizations, operations may be segmented into *divisions* covering the different activities in which the company is engaged, e.g. food, leisure and household goods. Each division is organized and administered as a separate operating unit, with its own cost centres, but treated overall as a *profit centre* because it has control over its pricing and marketing policies, and can therefore set its own profit targets.

When either a profit centre or a division has complete control over investment decisions affecting its operations, it is an *investment centre*. In these circumstances, whilst minimum targets of profit on capital employed are prescribed by head office, each division is treated as an autonomous unit.

Whether in charge of cost, profit or investment centres, managers will look to the management accounting system to provide relevant information to help them control their operations.

Essential characteristics of management accounting reports

Relevance

The importance of relevance is a recurring theme in connection with decision-making information and it is no less important with respect to control information. This implies that reports to different levels of management need only contain information appropriate to the decisions for which each manager is responsible.

For example, only at cost-centre level will *detailed* budget and actual comparisons be made in respect of each cost category. This is 'front-line' operational information, vital for day-to-day control.

Middle and top managers are primarily concerned with planning and therefore require only summarized information, sufficient to indicate whether plans need to be modified in the short term or radically reviewed for the long term.

Frequency

The timing of reports is mainly a function of the need to take action. For example, if excessive usage of a particular material is causing concern, a daily report might be desirable until the condition is corrected, especially if it is a particularly expensive material.

Direct labour is generally a high proportion of total cost, therefore justifies closer control than, say, the usage of stationery. Labour losses might require daily or even more frequent monitoring, whereas a monthly report on the cost of stationery will normally be quite adequate.

Routine reports produced at specified intervals should not be the only instruments of management control. *Ad hoc* inquiries and reports on critical areas which may initially be signalled by a routine report, are equally necessary to maintaining a dynamic quality in reporting.

Content

Reports should be designed to be easily read and understood – uncluttered by irrelevant detail. For example, a weekly report of all jobs by each worker may be completely disregarded by the responsible manager, as 'information overkill'. An efficiency report related to *total hours worked* by each employee should normally be quite adequate, and will at least stand a chance of being read.

The usefulness of reports will also be considerably enhanced if accompanied by interpretive explanations of the cold, bare figures.

Accuracy

Timeliness is of greater value than absolute accuracy in periodic reporting when decision-making cannot be delayed. This does not confer a licence on inefficient data gathering and analysis, it simply points out the importance of not taking the search for accuracy too far.

Noise

This term has its origins in the theory of communication systems (i.e. cybernetics), and refers to any factor that inhibits clear communication through all its stages of data collecting, recording, interpreting and transmitting.

A well-designed data processing system is a prerequisite, together with adequate internal checks to ensure the system handles only valid, complete data. Relevance of information transmitted has already been discussed, and this should go hand in hand with expert interpretation of reported information. Any 'noise' in the process of communication will render it less than effective.

Cost effectiveness

The cost of reporting should never exceed the estimated benefits arising from the information provided. The measure of this is to consider what loss might be suffered if a report were not made and then decide whether to produce a report that stems a possible loss at minimum cost.

So often, *ad hoc* reports called for by management become routine, when the need for the information has long since disappeared. This also has relevance to the cost/benefit implications of reporting deviations from plan, a topic covered later in this chapter.

DEPARTMENTAL OPERATING REPORT

PERIOD ....

DEPARTMENT ....

ACTIVITY: .... %

EFFICIENCY: .... %

CAPACITY: .... %

| YEAR TO DATE | DIRECT MATERIALS | PRODUCTION COST | | USAGE VARIANCE | % VARIANCE TO STANDARD |
		ACTUAL	STANDARD		
		£	£	£	
	P				
	Q				

| YEAR TO DATE | DIRECT LABOUR | ACTUAL WAGES PAID A | ACTUAL HRS AT STANDARD RATES B | HRS. PRODUCED AT STANDARD RATES C | VARIANCES | | % EFFICIENCY VARIABLE TO STANDARD |
					RATE A-B	EFFICIENCY B-C	
		£	£	£	£	£	
	C & P FINISHING						

| YEAR TO DATE | CONTROLLABLE OVERHEAD | ACTUAL COST | ALLOWED COST | | EXPENDITURE VARIANCE | % VARIANCE TO STANDARD |
			FIXED	VARIABLE		
		£	£	£	£	
	INDIRECT:					
	MATERIAL					
	LABOUR					
	EXPENSE					

| YEAR TO DATE | | ALLOWED COST A | OVERHEAD RECOVERED | | CAPACITY VARIANCE A-B | | EFFICIENCY VARIANCE B-C | |
			ACTUAL HOURS WORKED B	STANDARD HOURS PRODUCED C				
		£	£	£	£	%	£	%

Figure 21. Departmental operating report

Reporting to Management by Exception

The major difference between an accounting system that reports only actual performance, compared with one where comparisons are made between budgeted and actual performance, is that the recipient of the latter need only concentrate on significant variances between actual and plan. Whereas in an 'actual only' system, even when comparisons are made with last month or last year, every item will tend to be scrutinized – thereby diverting attention away from essential corrective action.

Comparing plan with actual invokes the principle of 'management by exception', putting the responsibility for control fairly and squarely on the shoulders of the responsible manager.

Departmental operating statements

These will be produced for 'front-line' managers, who operate the departments concerned with production, marketing, administration and finance.

As already explained, they will contain considerable detail on individual materials, labour and items of overhead expense, 'flexed' for the level of performance attained. Original budgets might be included in the statement if they still represent the overall target for the period.

A departmental operating statement produced, say, at four-weekly intervals is shown in Figure 21.

Reports, and more detailed explanations of material price, material usage and labour efficiency, may be produced at more frequent intervals to indicate where immediate corrective action is necessary. Specimen reports are illustrated in Figures 22, 23 and 24 below. Reasons for production overhead variances (see Chapter 14) should accompany the departmental operating statement.

				MATERIAL PRICE VARIANCE REPORT				
TO: PURCHASING MANAGER FROM: MANAGEMENT ACCOUNTANT					WEEK ENDED			
INVOICE DATE	SUPPLIER	MATERIAL	ACTUAL QUANTITY	VALUE AT STANDARD COST	VALUE AT ACTUAL COST	VARIANCE		EXPLANATION
						ADVERSE	FAV.	

Figure 22. *Material price variance report*

		MATERIAL USAGE VARIANCE REPORT						
DEPT..................							PERIOD................	
COST CENTRE	TYPE OF MATERIAL	QUANTITY		COST		VARIANCE		% ACTUAL TO STANDARD	EXPLANATION
		STANDARD	ACTUAL	STANDARD	ACTUAL	ADVERSE	FAV.	

Figure 23. *Material usage variance report*

	LABOUR EFFICIENCY REPORT							
DEPT.						PERIOD		
COST CENTRE AND JOB	HOURS			STANDARD RATE	VARIANCE		% ACTUAL TO STANDARD TIME	EXPLANATION
	STANDARD	ACTUAL	DIFF.		ADVERSE	FAV.	

Figure 24. *Labour efficiency report*

Selling and Administration Overhead

This will also be 'flexed' for performance attained, but in this instance for *sales* attained, not production. The major reasons for variances will be those caused by sales volume. Examples are: sales commission being directly related to the value of sales; unforeseen cost changes; greater or lesser efficiency in the use of the service provided; planning changes affecting discretionary costs such as advertising; and planning errors.

Functional management cost statements

Having delegated responsibility for controlling detailed costs to departmental managers, functional managers need only receive summaries of the total budgeted and actual costs of each cost centre under their separate control. They can always call for further back-up detail if it is required.

The format of these reports will vary with the type of operation, but will be in a form similar to the departmental operating statement illustrated above. The major difference will be that only *total* material, labour and overhead will be shown, instead of detailed expense items.

At this level, it is advisable to include the *original budget* for comparison, as decisions have to be made affecting production targets and achievements to date.

Profit and investment centre reports to top management

Top management will wish to be informed about revenue as well as costs, albeit in summary form; and, as regards investment centres, a comparison of planned and actual return on capital employed.

Exception reporting, in the form of consolidated variance profit and loss statements (illustrated at the end of Chapter 14) together with supporting explanatory detail, are a most effective way of informing management at this level.

Variance investigation

The decision to investigate a budget or standard costing variance, and then take action to correct its cause, is essentially a matter of weighing the costs of doing so against the possible benefits arising from taking corrective action. Investigation will cause extra expense, followed by the cost of corrective action if investigation reveals a condition worth correcting. In this respect, control limit charts can indicate when a variance is getting out of control.

Standards are set in the knowledge that they are, at best, averages of a range of possible cost outcomes. This being the case, unfavourable variances will be cancelled out by favourable ones within the limits of normally acceptable deviations. These are random, though acceptable, variances. Only when a variance falls outside these limits will it be worth investigating, and perhaps be controllable. Figure 25 illustrates variances, both within and outside control limits, the latter normally being determined by past experience.

The maintenance of these charts is a continuing investigative cost, but if a variance falls outside the control limits, management has to decide (a) whether to incur further investigative cost to unearth the cause, and (b) whether the present value of the net benefit of correcting the variance is greater than the cost of investigation, and therefore justifies the effort.

For example, if a favourable labour efficiency variance outside the control limits was to be repeated, say for

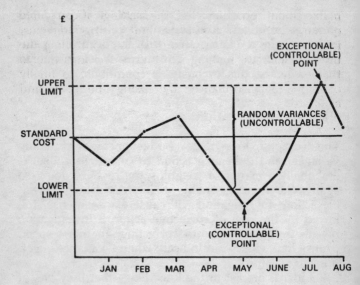

Figure 25. Variance control chart

three months, this could be an indication that the standard is too slack. Although favourable variances in themselves are not to be deplored, an excessive standard labour cost included in the make-up of a selling price could lead to loss of sales due to overpricing.

If investigation were to confirm that a wrong standard had been prescribed, the present value of additional sales resulting from a consequent drop in sales price might well exceed the cost of investigation and correction.

The management process completed

The process of correcting variances to keep the operational plan on course, brings us full circle through the management process from the setting of corporate objectives, through investment and pricing strategies, implementing the plan, recording and controlling the use of resources, making short-term decisions due to temporary changes in business conditions, to finally controlling performance by using budgets and standards.

Appendix:
Present value of £1

n Year	5%	6%	7%	8%	9%	10%	11%	12%	13%
0	1.000	1.000	1.000	1.000	1.000	1.000	1.000	1.000	1.000
1	.952	.943	.935	.926	.917	.909	.901	.893	.885
2	.907	.890	.873	.857	.842	.826	.812	.797	.783
3	.864	.840	.816	.794	.772	.751	.731	.712	.693
4	.823	.792	.763	.735	.708	.683	.659	.636	.613
5	.784	.747	.713	.681	.650	.621	.593	.567	.543
6	.746	.705	.666	.630	.596	.564	.535	.507	.480
7	.711	.665	.623	.583	.547	.513	.482	.452	.425
8	.677	.627	.582	.540	.502	.467	.434	.404	.376
9	.645	.592	.544	.500	.460	.424	.391	.361	.333
10	.614	.558	.508	.463	.422	.386	.352	.322	.295
11	.585	.527	.475	.429	.388	.350	.317	.287	.261
12	.557	.497	.444	.397	.356	.319	.286	.257	.231
13	.530	.469	.415	.368	.326	.290	.258	.229	.204
14	.505	.442	.388	.340	.299	.263	.232	.205	.181
15	.481	.417	.362	.315	.275	.239	.209	.183	.160
16	.458	.394	.339	.292	.252	.218	.188	.163	.141
17	.436	.371	.317	.270	.231	.198	.170	.146	.125
18	.416	.350	.296	.250	.212	.180	.153	.130	.111
19	.396	.331	.277	.232	.194	.164	.138	.116	.098
20	.377	.312	.258	.215	.178	.149	.124	.104	.087
25	.295	.233	.184	.146	.116	.092	.074	.059	.047
30	.231	.174	.131	.099	.075	.057	.044	.033	.026
35	.181	.130	.094	.068	.049	.036	.026	.019	.014
40	.142	.097	.067	.046	.032	.022	.015	.011	.008
45	.111	.073	.048	.031	.021	.014	.009	.006	.004
50	.087	.054	.034	.021	.013	.009	.005	.003	.002

Note: the above present value factors are based on year-end interest calculations.

14%	15%	16%	17%	18%	19%	20%	21%	22%	23%
1.000	1.000	1.000	1.000	1.000	1.000	1.000	1.000	1.000	1.000
.877	.870	.862	.855	.847	.840	.833	.826	.820	.813
.769	.756	.743	.731	.718	.706	.694	.683	.672	.661
.675	.658	.641	.624	.609	.593	.579	.564	.551	.537
.592	.572	.552	.534	.516	.499	.482	.467	.451	.437
.519	.497	.476	.456	.437	.419	.402	.386	.370	.355
.456	.432	.410	.390	.370	.352	.335	.319	.303	.289
.400	.376	.354	.333	.314	.296	.279	.263	.249	.235
.351	.327	.305	.285	.266	.249	.233	.218	.204	.191
.308	.284	.263	.243	.225	.209	.194	.180	.167	.155
.270	.247	.227	.208	.191	.176	.162	.149	.137	.126
.237	.215	.195	.178	.162	.148	.135	.123	.112	.103
.208	.187	.168	.152	.137	.124	.112	.102	.092	.083
.182	.163	.145	.130	.116	.104	.093	.084	.075	.068
.160	.141	.125	.111	.099	.088	.078	.069	.062	.055
.140	.123	.108	.095	.084	.074	.065	.057	.051	.045
.123	.107	.093	.081	.071	.062	.054	.047	.042	.036
.108	.093	.080	.069	.060	.052	.045	.039	.034	.030
.095	.081	.069	.059	.051	.044	.038	.032	.028	.024
.083	.070	.060	.051	.043	.037	.031	.027	.023	.020
.073	.061	.051	.043	.037	.031	.026	.022	.019	.016
.038	.030	.025	.020	.016	.013	.011	.009	.007	.006
.020	.015	.012	.009	.007	.005	.004	.003	.003	.002
.010	.008	.006	.004	.003	.002	.002	.001	.001	.001
.005	.004	.003	.002	.001	.001	.001	.000	.000	.000
.003	.002	.001	.001	.001	.000	.000	.000	.000	.000
.001	.001	.001	.000	.000	.000	.000	.000	.000	.000

Note: the above present value factors are based on year-end interest calculations.

n Year	24%	25%	26%	27%	28%	29%	30%	35%	40%
0	1.000	1.000	1.000	1.000	1.000	1.000	1.000	1.000	1.000
1	.807	.800	.794	.787	.781	.775	.769	.741	.714
2	.650	.640	.630	.620	.610	.601	.592	.549	.510
3	.524	.512	.500	.488	.477	.466	.455	.406	.364
4	.423	.410	.397	.384	.373	.361	.350	.301	.260
5	.341	.328	.315	.303	.291	.280	.269	.223	.186
6	.275	.262	.250	.238	.227	.217	.207	.165	.133
7	.222	.210	.198	.188	.178	.168	.159	.122	.095
8	.179	.168	.157	.148	.139	.130	.123	.091	.068
9	.144	.134	.125	.116	.108	.101	.094	.067	.048
10	.116	.107	.099	.092	.085	.078	.073	.050	.035
11	.094	.086	.079	.072	.066	.061	.056	.037	.025
12	.076	.069	.062	.057	.052	.047	.043	.027	.018
13	.061	.055	.050	.045	.040	.037	.033	.020	.013
14	.049	.044	.039	.035	.032	.028	.025	.015	.009
15	.040	.035	.031	.028	.025	.022	.020	.011	.006
16	.032	.028	.025	.022	.019	.017	.015	.008	.005
17	.026	.023	.020	.017	.015	.013	.012	.006	.003
18	.021	.018	.016	.014	.012	.010	.009	.005	.002
19	.017	.014	.012	.011	.009	.008	.007	.003	.002
20	.014	.012	.010	.008	.007	.006	.005	.002	.001
25	.005	.004	.003	.003	.002	.002	.001	.001	.000
30	.002	.001	.001	.001	.001	.000	.000	.000	.000
35	.001	.000	.000	.000	.000	.000	.000	.000	.000
40	.000	.000	.000	.000	.000	.000	.000	.000	.000
45	.000	.000	.000	.000	.000	.000	.000	.000	.000
50	.000	.000	.000	.000	.000	.000	.000	.000	.000

Note: the above present value factors are based on year-end interest calculations.

Index

Management

☐	**Effective Leadership**	John Adair	£2.50p
☐	**The Effective Executive**	} Peter Drucker	£1.95p
☐	**Management**		£3.95p
☐	**Under New Management**	Tony Eccles	£2.95p
☐	**Back from the Brink**	Michael Edwardes	£2.95p
☐	**How to Double Your Profits**	John Fenton	£2.50p
☐	**Inside Employment Law**	David Field	£2.50p
☐	**How to Win Customers**	Heinz Goldmann	£2.95p
☐	**Managing People at Work**	John Hunt	£2.50p
☐	**Investment Appraisal for Managers**	Graham Mott	£1.95p
☐	**Managing With Computers**	Terry Rowan	£2.95p
☐	**Guide to Saving and Investment**	James Rowlatt	£2.95p
☐	**Reality of Management**	} Rosemary Stewart	£1.95p
☐	**Reality of Organisations**		£1.95p
☐	**Bargaining for Results**	John Winkler	£2.50p
☐	**Multilingual Commercial Dictionary**		£3.95p

All these books are available at your local bookshop or newsagent, or can be ordered direct from the publisher. Indicate the number of copies required and fill in the form below

12
....

Name_____
(Block letters please)

Address_____

_____

Send to CS Department, Pan Books Ltd, PO Box 40, Basingstoke, Hants
Please enclose remittance to the value of the cover price plus:
35p for the first book plus 15p per copy for each additional book ordered
to a maximum charge of £1.25 to cover postage and packing
Applicable only in the UK

While every effort is made to keep prices low, it is sometimes
necessary to increase prices at short notice. Pan Books reserve
the right to show on covers and charge new retail prices which
may differ from those advertised in the text or elsewhere